"Can God raise the dead? W... ... transform a broken life? Read and see."

RICKY SKAGGS, *country music legend*

"You'll be amazed by these true stories where the impossible becomes possible. This book will give you the courageous faith of a lion."

DR. RICHARD BARTLETT

"Pastor Scarlett is one the most committed, unapologetic teachers of the Gospel of Jesus Christ that I have ever met. His enthusiasm for God and leading people into a life-changing relationship with Jesus is unique, powerful and contagious! I recommend that you read Pastor Dave Scarlett's book before Christ returns (which could be soon)!"

CLAY CLARK, *Host of the Thrivetime Show Podcast & Award-Winning Entrepreneur*

"Jesus is the God of the resurrection! This book will encourage your faith to receive resurrection power today."

PASTOR BRIAN GIBSON

"Do you believe in miracles? This book will open your eyes to what's possible with God"

DR. MARK SHERWOOD, *The Functional Medical Institute and Sherwood.TV*

"David's life is a marvel from start to finish. You will want to read this book with the earnest expectation that you will move to a place of greater love for the Father and His Glory."

PHIL HOTSENPILLER, *Senior Pastor, Influence Church*

"This true story is actually several amazing stories that will stir your faith. These true stories will stir your faith in God, and what He can do you your life. God has saved my life many times!"

PAUL E VALLELY, *Chairman of Stand Up America US Foundation MG US Army (Ret)*

ALL FOR HIS GLORY

THE NEAR-DEATH EXPERIENCE OF A MODERN-DAY JOB

DAVID SCARLETT

"The Lord gave, and the Lord has taken away;
Blessed be the name of the Lord."

—JOB 1:21

CONTENTS

THE END

"Are you ready, Dave?"

I can't answer the doctor. The breathing tube down my throat makes it impossible. It's also all that's keeping me alive. Am I ready for them to take it out? After all I've endured?

No, I'm not. But what are my choices?

Either I lie here and continue to wither or I asphyxiate as soon as they pull this tube. I think about my deepest, longest-held fear, the one that's haunted me since childhood: What if I die by drowning? That's got to be the worst way to go. To not be able to breathe? To not take in what I take for granted? To reach for what I know is freely available and yet not receive it?

"Dave, we're going to pull the tube." They say it like I agreed to it.

With a sound I never want to hear again, they remove the tube.

I desperately reach for what my body craves. But there's nothing. I can't breathe.

I hear machines scream their high-pitched warnings. I try again.

Still, nothing. I see panicked faces. It's got to be bad when the *doctors* look afraid.

And yet, as my worst fears are being realized, as I'm choking on nothingness and losing consciousness, I feel *fearless*. In fact, for the first time in months, I don't even feel pain. I've felt so much pain for so long that its absence astounds me.

And I know without a doubt: I'm dying.

The Lord—in his love, in his grace, and in his mercy—is removing all my fear, all my pain, and all my suffering.

In my darkest moment, I breathe in his light.

I close my eyes in this world and open them in the next.

When people hear that I've gone to heaven, their next question is understandable and inevitable: What's it like?

I give my honest answer, but I can't help but think about the apostle Paul's words describing the "third heaven," where he heard "inexpressible words" (2 Corinthians 12:2, 4). Or of Paul quoting Isaiah, saying how we just can't imagine what's truly in store for us because "eye has not seen, nor ear heard, nor have entered into the heart of man the things which God has prepared for those who love Him" (1 Corinthians 2:9).

How do you describe the indescribable? How do you contain eternity to a few words? How do you make finite the infinite? You can't. That's one thing Paul was getting at.

I will never be able to fully explain what happened to me, but here's what I experienced after I died. Blinding light surrounded me, so real and so heavy that I could feel it. An indescribable warmth radiated from within me. Peace descended upon me, a peace unlike any I've ever known. Unconditional love wrapped itself around me.

However you define *paradise*, whatever feelings and pictures may come to mind when you think about that word, multiply it by a thousand. Our earthly definitions of paradise fall far short of heaven's reality. There, your every sense is heightened. Sounds sound better.

Sights are astounding, even sparkling, radiating God's glory, his presence, his love, his peace, his hope.

What is heaven like? I'd never felt better in my life than in the two minutes I was technically dead.

The next question people tend to ask me is: Did you see your life flash before your eyes?

I did, but it didn't flash.

It felt like it took ten to fifteen minutes of heaven-time, if I can call it that. Since God exists outside of time and space, we can't say there's a one-to-one ratio of time on earth as it is in heaven. That's why I was dead for two minutes but experienced what felt like thirty minutes in heaven.

Put another way, God needed more than two minutes to reset my life.

I didn't see a time-lapse movie of my life. Rather, radiant photos in beautiful mahogany frames slowly passed by my eyes. The pictures were so clear and so detailed, better than any hi-def TV. The photos went chronologically, starting with me as a baby and then a toddler and so on, right up until my age of death at thirty-nine.[1]

As they went by and deep memories came up, I couldn't shake a strange feeling about these pictures. Suddenly, it dawned on me: this is the first time I've seen these photos. Yes, they were all true to my life, but they were all original. They were glimpses from God, his view of my life. What he wanted me to know about where I've been and where that would lead me.

As soon as I had that thought, I realized another important detail. No photo showed my moral failures. There was no record of wrongs

---

1 I would later see a biblical significance in my near-death at thirty-nine: The apostle Paul received "forty stripes minus one" (2 Corinthians 11:24) due to Jewish custom. And forty is often used in wilderness periods in the Bible. As you'll see, my wilderness period would begin as I turned forty.

to remind me of what I already knew of myself. There was grace in the absence of those memories because Jesus had washed my sins away.

I was grateful to realize this, but then I understood something upsetting: God hadn't counted my sin against me, but neither did I see any good for his glory remembered. In other words, my report card was empty. Up to that point in my life, I'd still been living for me. In that unforgettable moment in heaven, God asked me to live for him.

He said, "I'm going to send you back because I have a purpose for your life."

I said, "Whatever it is, Lord, I'll take it. I'll do whatever you want me to do."

He might as well have been asking me, "Are you ready, Dave?"

INTRODUCTION

Over the next many pages, we're going to get well acquainted. I'm going to share things with you that will feel far too personal—but some of my darkest times are already in the public record. In fact, my wife and I were featured on *The Steve Harvey Show* once. The segment was far from feel-good. You'll read more about that experience soon enough. In reliving the highs and lows of my life while writing the book, I can agree with Joseph's memorable words in Genesis 50:20: "You meant evil against me, but God meant it for good." My story is one of redemption in many, many ways.

Most people know me as Pastor Dave, the voice, founder, and leader of His Glory, a thriving online ministry that makes its home at hisglory.me.

- **Our purpose** is to spread the gospel from east to west to north to south, bringing the Word of His Glory to the world and allowing the His Glory family to find community and grow in their faith.
- **Our vision** is to reach a billion people worldwide with the hope of the gospel message and the truth of Jesus Christ.
- **Our mission** is to equip those who seek to bring light into the darkness, to perform prayer and baptism to those who are

called, to provide a platform to censored voices, and to support the poor around the globe with Bibles, food, and clothing.

We like to say that "His Glory was born to give people a future of hope," just as Jeremiah 29:11 says. And I remind both our viewers and myself about the world's great need for the gospel with the words I use to start every video: "We want to welcome all of His Glory nation, from east to west to north to south." Truly, we are reaching "the end of the earth" (Acts 1:8).

We accomplish this through daily video programs and annual revival tours that include biblical teachings, prayer, real news, interviews, and testimonies. We give a platform to pastors, prophetic voices, military leaders, politicians, and other brave patriots on the front lines fighting for God, truth, freedom, and justice.

But if you'd been able to tell twenty-year-old Dave that *that* would be his future, he would've laughed at you. Yet my mom knew. She always knew.

A Word about Prophetic Words

Debbie, my mother, is a devout Christian woman and a faithful prayer warrior. She also has the gift of prophecy. Throughout this book, you'll read and experience her prophetic words, words spoken from God's heart to hers, words that filled me with life and gave me an unerring faith in the goodness, the timeliness, and the power of God.

Even though I was raised in a Christian home, I was a typical teenager who became a typical young man. I wanted what the world offered over what my mom had long taught me about what God offers. You'll read those stories soon enough. Suffice it to say, I sought my own way. And since my own way worked for decades, I didn't see the need to ask for help from anyone, let alone God.

Like all good and godly moms, my mother allowed me to live my life, to make my own mistakes, to make my way in the world. All the while, she prayed. She nudged. She did her best to remind me of the truth that God's ways are so much better than ours if we'd just pay attention and give him control.

When I began my rapid ascent up the corporate ladder in the early 1990s, she handed me an Application Life Bible, a gift for my first big promotion to store manager at MC Sporting Goods in Kalamazoo, Michigan. But in those years I was too busy pursuing the American dream and the almighty dollar. I didn't have time for the Almighty himself. While my Bible collected dust, my mother gathered her hands in prayer every day on my behalf. For twenty-seven long years, as I wandered the wilderness of high-rises and higher salaries, she pleaded with God that he would become first in my life.

This book is a testament to her faithfulness. (And yes, I still have that Bible.)

I pray that her prophetic words, in context with the story of my life so far, inspire you the same way that they still inspire me.

Why I Wrote This Book

You could put this book down right now if you wholeheartedly believe this truth: heaven is real and God wants to meet you there when you die.

My ultimate goal in writing this book is to assure Christians of that fact, to add my voice to the chorus of so many others who've been blessed to die, to truly "taste and see that the Lord is good" (Psalm 34:8), and to return to this world to tell others about God's deep, eternal love. And if you're reading this book and you're not a Christian, my prayer is that God will spark his hope in your life, that he'll give you a glimpse through my story of just how powerful—and powerfully loving—he is.

If you get nothing else out of this book, bank this truth in the deepest part of your heart, mind, and soul. Just like Colton Burpo's famous book says, heaven *is* for real. My life, my *deaths*, and my new life all testify to that fact.

But I do hope you keep reading.

This book is my testimony. Of a husband challenged beyond the reasonable. Of a workaholic turned pastor. Of a dead man given true life.

THE FIRST TRIAL

CHAPTER 1

FIRST COMES LOVE

"And the Lord God said,
'It is not good that man should be alone.'"
—GENESIS 2:18

"It's a boy, Dave!"

You're not supposed to play favorites when it comes to expecting a child. Boy or girl, life is a gift from God. But if I'm honest with myself, when my wife Christine told me in early 2003 that we were going to have a boy, I was overjoyed. You can't know me for very long and not know a few facts: I love God, I love my family, I love sports, and I love the University of Michigan. As soon as she told me she was pregnant with our first child together, a *son*, I had visions of him as QB1 for the Wolverines.

But I also had more realistic dreams. I thought about the legacy handed to me that I hoped to one day hand to my son—a warrior legacy of courage. I never met my mother's father, Lt. Col. Kenneth

Chamberlain (USMC), but I know he was a hero. A fighter pilot in World War II and the Korean War with Marine Fighter Attack Squadron 323, a.k.a. the "Death Rattlers," he survived when hundreds of thousands more didn't. Like so many men of that era, men who witnessed unspeakable tragedies, he rarely spoke about his time in combat. Which also meant he rarely spoke about his heroics. From all reports, he was a humble man who capably served his country. My family likely would never have known about his courage and bravery if his war buddies hadn't told so many stories during his funeral. And I wouldn't have such a warrior legacy coursing through my veins.

A legacy I knew would also course through my son's blood.

On September 22, 2003, we welcomed Jagger into our family.

I felt as blessed and fortunate as the day Christine and I first met.

She made the first move.

Nobody believes me when I tell them this, especially if they know Christine. She's quiet, unassuming. She's beautiful, but she doesn't purposefully seek out attention. On the night we met, she certainly attracted mine.

In 1998 I was a market manager in northern Michigan for AirTouch Cellular, which would eventually become Vodafone/Verizon Wireless. When I walked into the company Christmas party, I saw Christine across the way. Just like in a movie, time slowed and everyone else in the room seemed to fade away. I just saw her: brunette hair, a vibrant smile, a radiating inner beauty.

But I didn't approach, for at least two reasons: nerves and ethics. In some ways, I felt like I was in the fifth grade again, about to ask a cute girl to dance who I knew would, *at best*, flatly say no. I was afraid to be embarrassed, especially as a higher-ranking manager in the company.

My position was also a problem. Christine's boss reported to me. And I didn't date employees. I laughed to myself as I considered the irony of the situation before me. When I was a teenager, I'd had a steady relationship with my high school sweetheart—and her dad was my boss at the local car dealership. Now I was the boss with ethical decisions to make. So I stayed on my side of the room, just me and all the other guys too stuck in their fifth-grade minds to man up and just talk to a girl.

Then she started walking toward me. No, it wasn't walking. She glided. The music to the movie in my memories crescendoed until she stood before me. Then all noise, all feeling, all sight outside of her faded. This vision of a woman before me looked me in the eye and smiled.

She said, "You're good-looking."

I was shocked, both by her closeness and her directness. I didn't know what to say. The silence was painful. Even though my heart was racing, I kept my composure—I think. Stunned and flattered, all I could do was blurt out what I'd been thinking before she'd walked over: "I can't date employees."

She mentioned that she'd quit if needed.

Then I asked, "Would you like to dance right now?" (Fifth-grade me would have been so proud.)

She smiled and grabbed my hand. We danced for a couple of hours. We talked about what had brought us together. As the event ended, Christine approached me to say goodbye, then she walked toward the exit. I hurried to meet her before she left and asked her to wait so we could leave together. Neither of us could deny that a strong connection was forming.

By the time we left, I knew I'd have to deeply wrestle with the ethics of dating an employee. I wanted to see her again and again. I wanted to talk to her every day. I wanted to know her life story, and I wanted our life stories to join together. I was pretty sure I wanted to marry her.[2]

My ethical problem soon resolved itself. Again, Christine made the first move. She quit her job, just like she'd said she would. After just a few months of courtship, we took a cruise to Cozumel.[3] I proposed to Christine at the city's gates. I told her, "I've never done this before. Will you marry me?" We married on January 28, 2000.

That's the day I also became a stepfather.

Brittney was a toddler when Christine and I married, a child from Christine's previous marriage. And Brittney was an adorable, precious, two-year-old little girl. I was thrilled to become her stepfather.

Christine had just recently divorced. I knew she'd fought to save her marriage, but her ex-husband hadn't chosen reconciliation. I also understood the difficulties of that time for her, and especially as a single parent. We both knew the detrimental effects that divorce can have for the children involved, and she never wanted to go through her divorce for that reason. Still, she valiantly raised her daughter by herself while also trying to figure out what had gone wrong in her previous marriage. So when we met and subsequently married, I have to imagine that a heavy weight lifted from her shoulders. She would no longer have to bear the burden of single parenting or spend nights

---

2   Months later, I'd learn that a couple of ladies had been matchmaking us that night.
3   We didn't like the cruise, but we loved Cozumel so much that we vacation there every year.

where her only conversation partner was a baby. We became Team Scarlett.

Unfortunately, I'd been long acquainted with the challenges of divorce. Although I'd never been married until I met Christine, I knew firsthand how difficult divorce could be. I knew divorce had destroyed many families because I'd witnessed it in my childhood. I often thought how unfair it was to the children, how a family separating could detrimentally affect the ones who'd done nothing to deserve such an upheaval to their lives.

But I also knew the pains of divorce on a deeper level. When I was five, my parents divorced—and that was during a time when divorce was far from as prevalent as it is today. Consequently, my mother primarily raised me, and I never had a close relationship with my father while growing up.

Both of my parents remarried in time, and each new stepparent brought new siblings into my life. My mother married Bruce Smith, a Michigan State Trooper. They had Geoff, a new half-brother, an incredibly funny man whom I'm still close to today and who works with me in ministry. My father remarried and he and his wife had two daughters, Laura and Heather. I was grateful for our growing family.

Although we were thoroughly middle class, my parents ensured that we didn't suffer want. We may not have eaten out much, but going to McDonald's was a big treat. In my entire childhood, we may have only eaten there four or five times. My stepdad gave us a budget of $1 so I had to decide between my favorite burger or a budget burger. Though my stomach longed for a quarter-pounder with cheese, the plain cheeseburger won out because it was more value for my money.

Our family may have been broken in the traditional sense, but I look back on my childhood with gratitude. Having so many siblings helped ease the loneliness. But my mom was always the glue holding us together, her prayers and faithfulness guiding our way. Without her deep influence on my life, I truly don't know how my life would have turned out.

I say all that to say this: I felt empathy for the loss Christine had endured in her divorce. And I understood Brittney's hesitance to accept me on day one. So I did my best to make her adjustment to a new family as easy as possible.

In fact, having an instant family, so to speak, sparked my search for a church. Christine had grown up Catholic. I'd grown up Baptist. With a toddler we wanted to raise right and our hopes of one day expanding our family, I knew we needed to find a church home.

We attended a Lutheran church for a time, but it didn't feel like a home church. We also noticed that many of the area pastors were preaching "replacement theology" instead of teaching that the Bible is the infallible Word of God. These pastors were good people, but we didn't agree with their theology. So we kept searching. In hindsight, I know now that God was revealing crucial truths about the church to me during this time in our lives. But I was still so self-focused on my career that I didn't fully appreciate what he was trying to teach me in that season until years later.

The search for a new church eventually led us to our own Bible studies, and specifically the online studies of Chuck Missler. Even then, God was planting the seeds for the online ministry at His Glory that he would eventually call us to. But our family would have to endure many trials and tribulations before the ministry was born.

CHAPTER 2

WORKING MAN

"Unless the Lord builds the house, They labor in vain who build it … It is vain for you to rise up early, To sit up late, To eat the bread of sorrows; For so He gives His beloved sleep."

—PSALM 127:1–2

In the days before I knew Truth and followed his plan for my life, I knew one truth for certain: I could outwork *any* problem. I knew this to be true because my resume revealed it.

As a teenager in Michigan, I worked hard to become the quarterback for the Lakeview High School Wildcats. Central and Northern Michigan both recruited me with football scholarships. Despite my love of the game, I turned down their offers in order to join the Marines and serve my country. Boot camp and my time in service truly taught me both the value of hard work and the mental and physical stamina that's necessary for doing your best in trying circumstances. The Marines also instilled within me a burning passion to be the best of the best. As a young man fresh out of the service, I didn't just want to climb the corporate ladder. I wanted to be the fastest to ever scale it.

When I was twenty years old, I worked for my father's insurance company. That's when business became my passion and Sam Walton became my inspiration. As the founder of Walmart and Sam's Club, he knew more than a thing or two about what I most wanted to succeed in: the business of making money. I devoured his books, ingesting his genius as much as I could. I still believe that his words of wisdom catapulted my career beyond what was typical for my age.

It's no wonder that I applied an "outwork" mentality to all of my life. In his biography, Walton wrote, "You can make a positive out of most any negative if you work at it hard enough. I've always thought of problems as challenges."[4] If it worked for Sam, shouldn't it work for me?

I soon left my father's company and applied to be a salesperson at MCSports in Flint, Michigan. It was part of the eighty-store chain MC Sporting Goods. Believe it or not, my early work there mainly consisted of cleaning toilets. I guess I hadn't read the fine print of my salesperson contract to know that that was one of my job responsibilities. But I also didn't care. Even though the work wasn't glorious, I knew that I could work my way up the ranks if I just did *any* job well and with a good attitude. I was on the lowest rung of the corporate ladder when I started, but I showed up every day and worked hard to be the best salesperson I could be. In fact, I literally lived off of eggs and bread during a particularly meager financial stretch. But my dedication eventually paid off and I became a store manager. Inspired

---

4 **"I've always thought of problems as challenges"**: Sam Walton and John Huey, *Sam Walton, Made in America: My Story* (United Kingdom: Random House Publishing Group, 1993), 39.

by Walton's words of managerial wisdom, I helped take that store to be the best in its chain of a hundred stores statewide.

Buoyed by my success, I wanted more: more responsibility, more respectability, more bankability. I left MCSports after five years to become a general manager at OfficeMax. At twenty-five years old, I became a director over both Michigan and Indiana. I'm reminded of more from Sam: "If you love your work, you'll be out there every day trying to do it the best you possibly can, and pretty soon everybody around will catch the passion from you—like a fever."[5]

I loved my work. I'd like to think that my drivenness, my desire for excellence, and my genuine joy to lead others were infectious. That others truly did "catch the passion" from me. After six years with OfficeMax, I left for Verizon. I quickly rose from a market manager to a district manager. Our company won awards. Our team won accolades. I was all of thirty years old and living my dream. In fact, the dream just kept getting better because this is when my dream girl stepped into my life.

A few months after I married Christine, my success at Verizon helped me land a huge promotion at AT&T. I'd be their youngest director in the country, overseeing the Ohio and Michigan markets. Amazingly, AT&T hired me despite my lack of a college degree. At the time, I was the only director to ever have been awarded that role without having earned a degree. They made an exception for me based on my track record. But they didn't let me off so easily.

Since AT&T had certain standards to uphold for their hiring, especially for upper-level roles, they asked that I pursue a college degree in my off time. As a go-getter unafraid of a challenge, and as someone who didn't mind hard work, I enrolled for online classes through Almeda College to complete the bachelor's degree I'd begun

5 **"If you love your work"**: Walton, 314.

at Kalamazoo College (which I'd had to defer because of my time in the Marines). Thankfully, because of my time in the Marines, the GI bill covered my costs. In 2004, I earned a bachelor's in business administration with the help of the HR director at OfficeMax.

The job change also required a location change from Michigan, where each of us had grown up, to Ohio, a completely new state for both of us. We'd be without the family and friends we loved in Michigan, but I vainly believed we'd be OK since we now had each other to lean on. Plus, because I was sold out to work, I truly didn't think much of the move. If uprooting our lives was what the job required, I'd have the moving truck in our garage the next day. That's what the paycheck demanded. That's what my constant drive for success warranted. So we moved. I know Christine wasn't excited about it because she was very close with her family and had spent much of her time with her sisters. But she also knew it was what we needed to do to start our new family.

It's easy to look back on the months before your most challenging trials and tribulations and ask, "What if?"

What if we hadn't moved?

What if we had found a strong church home?

What if I had been less focused on myself?

What if I'd worked fewer hours, been more present, been more prayerful?

Would it have changed the catastrophe around the corner?

After our move, Christine put on a happy face—happy for my success, happy for our new life together, but not exactly excited. She wanted stability and consistency, but our first few years as a married couple were filled with nonstop change and growth, mostly as a result of my drive for more. We were still in our honeymoon phase, but if I'd paid better attention, maybe I would have seen the doubt hiding at the corners of her smile.

So when she told me that she was applying to be a substitute teacher at the local elementary school, I celebrated her decision. She has such a caring demeanor that I knew teaching could be her calling, a place where she could make a difference as well as rid herself of the loneliness that had been nagging at her since our move. The only disappointment was that the elementary had no available positions for substitutes at that time, but the high school did. I could tell that she wasn't thrilled with teaching teenagers, but she still accepted the job and was eager to begin.

When we moved, she knew she'd be far from friends and family. She didn't know how far she'd be from me. Yes, we were together in those early days, just two lovebirds getting to know each other, learning how to live with one another, and raising a daughter together. But my idol was work, and I served it dutifully and often. I believed the lie that just a few more hours at work were always justified because I was providing for my family. In reality, looking back, I worked long hours because it made me feel good about myself. Important. Valued. Worthy. Not to mention, there was always a monetary equivalent to it. I could see just how much I was truly worth every time I checked my growing bank account.

But I was discontent. No amount of work or money was ever going to fill the God-shaped hole at the center of my soul. As a young man with a new wife and child, I didn't know that then. I just thought, *This is what men do, right?*

Because I found success in work, I found my value in work. I defined myself by the titles I held: director, manager, boss. That I was so comparatively young and yet so high on the corporate ladder made me all the prouder. As Walton wrote, "It never occurred to me that I might lose; to me, it was almost as if I had a right to win."[6]

I won and I won and I won.

Until I nearly lost it all.

6 **"never occurred to me that I might lose"**: Walton, 18.

CHAPTER 3

CONFESSION

*"Your hands have made me and fashioned me, An intri-
cate unity; Yet You would destroy me."*

—JOB 10:8

"We need to talk, Dave."

No one *ever* wants to hear those four words. Rarely do they ever mean anything other than something serious, upsetting, tragic, or all of the above. When you hear those words, your fight-or-flight response kicks into high gear. Most people want to run. They steel themselves for what's about to come.

When Christine told me "We need to talk" three months after Jagger's birth, I knew it was serious. Ever since the move to Ohio, we hadn't truly been *us*. I blamed it on my long work hours and her distance from friends and family. Christine had also been seeing a marriage counselor around this time. She'd asked me to accompany her, but I didn't believe the counselor could help. Plus, my schedule didn't have the margin for any more meetings.

But I couldn't deny that we just hadn't been clicking or talking like we used to, even just a few months ago. I'd known something was off with our relationship, but I'd repeatedly convinced myself to remain quiet about it. If there was a can of worms in our relationship, I didn't want to be the one to open it.

But the way she said "We need to talk" made my heart sink. *Is it really this bad?* My stomach ached as I knew she was about to tell me something terrible.

I had no idea just how bad it was.

The setting was mundane but appropriate. She was giving Jagger a bath and asked me to come to the bathroom. We started discussing our days, a normal night like any other. But this night would change our normal for years to come.

With tears forming in her eyes, she looked into mine. For the briefest of moments, I saw the eyes I'd gotten so lost in at the Christmas party just a few years ago. And what happened then was happening right now: time stood still, pregnant with possibility. My peripheral vision went fuzzy, narrowing to focus only on her.

"Dave . . . ."

I don't speak. I can tell this is painful for her, but I also don't know what to say. I can only think about the distance that's grown between us in just a few short months. I feel a quick pang of remorse for the hours I've been working during the day and the hours I've been studying at night. If she says she's upset with me for not being around enough for her, I don't have an argument. She's right. Before she says another word, I tell myself that I'm not going to work as much, that I'll make more time for her and Brittney. I start devising a plan but—

"Jagger may not be yours."

My eyes go wide.

Christine sees my confusion. "He may not be your biological son."

My stomach drops. My heart hurts. I put my head in my hands. I don't say anything. I start to ask, "Who's the—" but I cut myself off. I don't want to know. Not right now. Answers can wait.

I'm about to be a college graduate. I'm a former Marine and a Fortune 100 manager at just thirty-five years old. I have won and won and won. But nothing's prepared me for this.

This isn't supposed to happen.

So what's supposed to happen next?

In the days following her admission to an affair, I withdrew. I didn't want to see my wife. I didn't want to talk to her. Despite my mind trying to guess details, I didn't want to know any. I didn't want to know who she'd been seeing either. I didn't sleep. I barely ate.

When I wasn't wondering how I'd been so blind to what had been happening for six to eight months, just running away from the problems in my work, my thoughts were consumed with *What do I do now?* I didn't believe in divorce, but I also wondered just how much pain a man could bear before divorce was a viable option. I tried to work but couldn't focus. Home was no different. I was restless and angry, sad and confused. For the first time in my life, I didn't know what to do or who to turn to. Who could help me in a tragedy like this?

So I prayed. Like a man drowning in the ocean, I prayed. I asked God for guidance, wisdom, and discernment. *Just tell me what to do, Lord.* I thought about my long history of only turning to God in the hard times. When I was young, I wasn't interested in the Bible. I went to church because my parents made me. I was what many would call a "911 Christian." If I was in an emergency, I knew I could ring up God and he'd answer because he had to. That was one of his jobs, right? In the days and months after Christine confessed to me, I felt as helpless as a child. In all my prayers, I wondered if my Father was picking up. The other end of the line certainly sounded silent.

Then one day in my distress, I saw a large, dusty black book on my shelf. I picked it up, wiped it off, and opened the Bible my mom had given me after my first promotion. That's the day her many years of prayers on my behalf, as countless as the dust particles on that Bible, came to fruition. In his infinite wisdom and mercy, God knew I'd need him and the truth of his Word to keep me from drowning in sorrow and anguish. That's the day God's Word forever became my life preserver.

Not long after that, Christine and I finally spoke again for what seemed like the first time in several days. That's when I got the full picture of what had happened. It was far worse than my original fears. What she shared shocked me even more than her admission to an affair. What she told me had never even entered my mind as a possibility. So when Christine told me whom she'd had the affair with, I went numb.

"Jagger's dad . . . ." She trailed off, tears forming.

I sat silently.

" . . . is a senior at the high school."

Imagine the worst sin in your life. Then imagine that sin being made headline news. And then imagine that news lasting not for months or years but for the rest of your life. The headlines are still online:

- "Teacher gets three days in jail for sex with student"
- "Ex-teacher who had student's baby sentenced"
- "Former Student Fights Teacher for Custody of Their Son"

This is the hell my wife endured. This is the hell we lived in for three years. Notoriety of a sort we never could have imagined and never would have willingly brought upon ourselves or anyone else. Christine admitted the affair to me in January 2004. She was criminally charged in 2006 with sexual battery and sentenced in 2007.

Once the truth of the affair came to light, Christine didn't shy away from admitting her wrongdoing and trying to do the right thing. In fact, Christine shared our story as a caution to other women on *The Steve Harvey Show* for an episode that aired on January 26, 2016. A one-minute-and-thirty-four-second clip of that episode is available online.[7] It provides a glimpse into Christine's world during this tumultuous time as well as her forthrightness when it came to discussing what had happened.

Steve Harvey: "OK, so what made you actually turn to this student?"

Christine Scarlett: "Part of the reason, we did move to a different state, and all of a sudden I was without friends, family, and I was alone. My husband was pretty much a workaholic, and I came from a very troubled childhood. I was very, very needy. So I think that unfortunately there was an immature part of me that ate up the attention. And so if someone could wonder why somebody could do something like this, it's shameful to admit, but yeah, there was a void in my life that I think it filled. And I hope that other women might hear that. It's nothing you want to mess with. It's not a path you want to go down."

---

7   The Steve Harvey **Show clip:** News 5 Cleveland. n.d. "TODAY on STEVE HARVEY," https://www.facebook.com/News5Cleveland/videos/10154573207729922.

Steve: "Yeah, absolutely. Let me ask you this. What happened when you found out you were pregnant?"

Christine: "Well, I was overjoyed that I was pregnant, but it did entertain my mind that—"

Steve: "Wait, wait, wait. You were overjoyed that you were pregnant?"

Christine: "Yeah. I thought it was my husband and . . . our baby."

Steve: "Oh, I see what you're saying."

Christine: "No, I did not know. Actually, it entered my mind it could be, but I really brainwashed myself into believing that it was our child."

Steve: "Uh-huh, oh, OK, I got you."

Christine: "So, and just a life, growing in me, I mean, you know, I was overjoyed with it. So, it didn't . . . nothing troubled me until the child was about three months old. You know, pulling him out of the bathtub after a bath and just, it dawning on me that the child resembled the student."

Not everyone is as nice as Steve Harvey though.

Because of the salaciousness of the story, Christine was often vilified by the news. Her words were taken out of context or twisted or exaggerated. She cried herself to sleep most nights.

But in her darkest moments, the Lord of light showed up. Just as God had rekindled my faith, God was also working in the deepest, darkest recesses of Christine's heart to heal hurts she'd had since childhood. Christine's mother was all of eighteen years old when Christine was born, which meant that Christine was forced to fend for herself from an early age. When she was five, her parents went through a bitter divorce that separated the five siblings. Christine was effectively forced to grow up fast and alone. She often felt lost. It's too simple to say that the wounds of her childhood resulted in her pursuing an affair as an adult. But it's also undeniable that her abandonment and loneliness for so long played a factor in this tragedy. My absence due to an addiction to work and success only increased her hidden burden.

During the hardest times after her affair was made public, Christine fought herself every night, wondering if someone like her could be forgiven for such a catastrophic sin. Over time, she would learn and savor the truth of Romans 8:39: Nothing "shall be able to separate us from the love of God which is in Christ Jesus our Lord."

She suffered the consequences of her actions. She accepted responsibility for what she did. But what's most important is that she accepted God's forgiveness.

The world condemned her. Her heavenly Father forgave her.

Could I?

CHAPTER 4

MY SON, MY SON

"For I know the thoughts that I think toward you, says the Lord, thoughts of peace and not of evil, to give you a future and a hope."
—JEREMIAH 29:11

"Jagger's dad was here."

I heard Christine's words but they didn't register. *I'm Jagger's dad,* I thought. Then, *He was in our house?*

She must have seen my confusion. "He wanted to take a picture of Jagger."

In a flash, the full reality of our situation struck me. This other man was Jagger's dad. Not only that, but if Christine and I stayed together, we would have to work with him for decades to ensure that Jagger had all he needed for a healthy, full life. Jagger was the only innocent party in our mess.

I put my head in my hands. I thought about when Christine first told me the full story. Everything within me wanted to be done with the chaos. I cried and prayed and started devouring the Word of God. After days of praying and crying out to the Lord, he gave me the peace to fight. He impressed upon me that if he can take it to the cross for all my sins, then I should have the same forgiveness.

He led me to learn everything about King David. I saw how David had committed adultery and had ordered Uriah's murder, but still David turned all his sin to the Lord and the Lord forgave him. God even called him his beloved. It's a staggering story in so many ways.

But forgiveness is often a daily choice. When Christine told me Jagger's dad had been at our house and my anger flared again, everything within me wanted to run, to be done with what my daily life had become. I was exhausted, and I was exhausted of being exhausted. Again, with nowhere to turn but to God in prayer, I asked for his guidance. "Am I supposed to stay with Christine, Lord? I'm in so much pain, and this affair is so public and sordid. I can't outwork this problem. It's too big for me to handle. I don't even know where to start. All I know is that I want out. But what would you have me do?"

I waited, honestly not expecting a quick reply. But then I heard a single firm word of undeniable strength and certainty: "Stay."

Relief flooded through my weary soul. His peace that passes understanding passed through me. For the first time in months, I slept well. Although I knew the road before us would be the most difficult challenge we'd ever face, I had the firm conviction that we were meant to travel that road together.

So I stayed.

In fact, of the twenty-eight couples that Steve Harvey interviewed for the show we would eventually go on, we were the only couple who had stayed together. The only reason that had been possible was because of God's grace and the fact that *both* Christine and I chose to put God at the center of our lives as he rebuilt our marriage in the midst of immense wreckage.

We both knew we'd messed up. And we also both loved Jagger and wanted the best for him. So we began the slow process of allowing God to heal our broken hearts and then to mend our marriage. As we told our families about our decision to remain together, they honored us with their prayers for our health, for our unity, and for our spiritual lives. I firmly believe that their prayers often carried our burdens to the foot of the cross and allowed Christine and me to experience immense spiritual growth even during such a dark time.

Personally, I began reading the Bible daily, a first for me. God routinely revealed to me how his timeless truth related to my situation. I understood my complicity in what had occurred. I wasn't a blameless party. I saw how my inattentiveness at home and my singular focus on work had helped to create an environment in which the Enemy could thrive in his deceptions.

Now, imagine a triangle with a husband at one base and his wife at the other. God is at the top. If both the husband and wife seek God, they can't help but grow closer together. By placing God first in our lives, even above each other, we rediscovered our marriage. With time and through prayer, Christine and I found our way back to each other. Yes, we would fight trust issues for years, but God's firm word would always remind me: "Stay."

As our home life grew stronger, it seemed that everything else was falling apart. We were being sued both in criminal court and in civil court. As a result, our life savings were quickly dwindling. We were also battling for Jagger after his biological father demanded a DNA test and sought custody, an experience that caused a deep emotional toll on both of us. And Christine faced the prospect of jail time, something I couldn't fathom when we had just truly reconnected as husband and wife.

Honestly, I felt like Job from the Bible, catastrophe after catastrophe after catastrophe. I could agree with what he'd written so long ago: "The Lord gave, and the Lord has taken away" (Job 1:21). And in all this loss, I finally lost what had long been my most treasured possession.

AT&T fired me.

In an alternate 2004, I became a high-level executive at AT&T/Vodaphone. After all, Vodaphone's CEO was a good friend of mine. Before the merger, he told me he had plans for me, that I could bank on a promotion to the upper ranks. After the merger, I relished having my dream job. I'd finished my speed race of a climb up the corporate ladder. I was at the pinnacle of worldly success, making more money than I'd ever imagined. Everything that I had raced so hard and so long to achieve was mine.

But that's not what happened.

On October 26, 2004, Cingular Wireless acquired AT&T Wireless. The acquisition caught us all off-guard. The sudden firings were even more shocking. In the midst of the costly criminal, civil, and custody trials that Christine and I were fighting, I was fired. In less than twenty-four hours everything had changed: my only source of comfort, security, and identity had been taken away from me. In the moment, I was shocked and confused bust mostly angry. *How could they*? I thought. In hindsight, I know God was moving the chess pieces of my life so he could become my King.

With a business story that made national news, the Lord had taken away my central idol. With more time on my hands, less focus on the success of the world, and the weight of our literal trials on my shoulders, I sought God's voice. I didn't just pray. I asked God to speak. I wanted to hear from him. I was a desperate man in desperate need.

Finally, God picked up my call.

I'll never forget the first time I heard God speak: "My hand is upon you and your family, and you will pull through this and be stronger as a family."

I wanted to believe, but my growing faith still had seeds of doubt. Soon thereafter, I was waiting for my wife at a restaurant. She wasn't due to arrive until some time later. So I humbly asked God for confirmation of his words to me. "Would you send Christine through the door next to let me know I truly heard from you yesterday?"

Sure enough, Christine appeared a moment later. She might as well have been wearing Gideon's fleece around her shoulders. Never before that moment had I been so bold as to ask God to confirm his voice to me. But I would never hesitate to do so for the rest of my life.

In fact, confirmation of God's voice speaking into my life would begin to come regularly from a source I'd long trusted and loved deeply.

On May 27, 2005, my mother Debbie shared the following prophetic word with me. It would be the first of many that still continue today. I smile with gladness and a deep sense of gratitude for my mother's faithfulness through all the trials I endured. And, in reading back through these prophetic words, I'm awed by God's nearness and lovingkindness in providing my family with such specific encouragement during some of the most difficult times of our lives.

> My Son,
>
> Have you not heard? I, the Lord, am your high tower.
>
> Your cries reach out to me and my heart grieves with your heart. Sin always is destructive, that is why I gave my commandments. They are not given to bind, but to protect my loved ones from hurt.

Seek me with all your heart, and you will find me. For I know the plans I have for you, not for harm, but to prosper you, to give you a future, and hope.

Walk with me my son, and I will bless, and I will supply. I will restore everything the evil one has stolen from you. This world belongs to the evil one, your home is on high. My saints continue to battle as my warriors . . . for they know the cost is high. Each soul is precious to me. How I long for people to know their God, the one true God.

Life is a test, who will turn to me, who will be devoted to me, who will follow my will?

I AM that I AM! There is none like me! I am the alpha and the omega. I know the beginning and the end. There is nothing I long for more, than to have intimacy with you, my son.

Read my Word, soak me in, and I will reveal the secrets of my kingdom.

David, a name after my precious servant. It is a strong name, you will be a leader like King David. I will use you mightily in my kingdom. I love you, my son.

Your Father

In this tumultuous but spiritually fulfilling time of my life, I felt like the father who sought out Jesus because his son was possessed and thrown into seizures. The father asks Jesus, "If you can do anything, take pity on us and help us" (Mark 9:22).

Jesus replies, "If you can? Everything is possible for one who believes" (v. 23).

And the father speaks a truth I often felt during these years: "I do believe; help me overcome my unbelief" (v. 24).

Then, of course, Jesus performs a miracle and heals the man's son.

In the aftermath of God speaking to me, he would perform miracles in our lives as well.

"It's a boy, Dave!"

In 2006, Christine told me we were pregnant, except she hadn't told me it would be a boy. In fact, during this time of my life, as she and I were growing both closer together and closer to the Lord, I was hearing more from God—and God told me that we were going to have a boy who should be named Creed William, after my paternal grandfather.[8]

Creed William was born on February 7, 2007. God told me that his namesake, who'd passed away years earlier, was pleased with the honor of our Creed being named after him. Still, in these early years of my spiritual growth, I doubted whether what I was hearing was truly from God. So I humbly asked again for confirmation that it was his truth I was hearing. "Lord, please let me know if this is from you."

I went to bed with my thoughts racing. *Christine can't go to jail. She just can't. We've come so far. And now a son! What will Brittney, Jagger, Creed, and I do if Christine has to serve time? How will I be able to work and care for them all? Will Christine be OK? Will we get custody of Jagger? What headline am I going to wake up to tomorrow? When will this end, Lord? Still, I know you are with us. Calm my soul. Let me know you hear my prayer.*

---

8 In fact, this experience echoed a moment in my mother's life shortly after I was born. She told me that her departed father, a lieutenant colonel pilot in the Marines, had visited her in a dream and said, "He's beautiful."

Exhausted, I fell asleep until—BAM!

My alarm clock read 3:00 a.m. The noise was so loud that I thought an airplane had crashed through our top-story bathroom. I jumped out of bed and ran upstairs. I opened the door to the bathroom and saw nothing out of order. No airplane parts. No broken pipes. Nothing. I peeked in on the kids to see if they had been up to something, but they were both sleeping soundly. I didn't see anything broken or fallen elsewhere in the house.

And then I remembered: *confirmation*. In the still of the night, God reminded me that he was indeed listening. In three months, I would need to lean as heavily as ever on my heavenly Father. Christine's sentencing was rapidly approaching.

CHAPTER 5

GOD OF RESTORATION

"The Lord restored Job's losses . . . . Indeed the Lord gave Job twice as much as he had before."

—JOB 42:10

On February 16, 2006, as Christine and I were still wrestling with our situation, my mother sent me this prophetic word:

Be at peace, Debbie about Dave's situation. It is a great testing for him, but he will overcome, and become strong, not strong physically, but STRONG IN ME.

I have a purpose for his life. I will use him mightily but first he must go through the fiery furnace, so he will be unquenchable for me. I use those who have been severely tested, but trust in me through it all. I know that I can trust them and use them for mighty things.

Never doubt that I have my hand on him, and his situation. Did you not surrender them to me? Watch, beloved, how your son will overcome and be used by me. He will know me intimately . . . his is a high call. I am purifying him.

Beloved, know I am with you all.

As Christine and I awaited her sentencing in court, our families were there with us. In fact, we all prayed together before the sentence came down. We expected that Christine would be sent to prison for seventeen years.

After all the progress that we'd made in our marriage, I truly didn't want to consider the possibility of our separation. Not now. Not when our lives seemed to be going in the right direction, even despite the chaos that surrounded us. When the judge opened his mouth to deliver her judgment, I held my breath.

When the judge spoke, neither Christine nor I could believe our ears. She was sentenced to three days in jail, 180 days of home detention, 300 hours of community work service, financial restitution for the victim's counseling, and probation. Christine told the victim, "From the bottom of my heart, I am extremely sorry for hurting you and your family. I will always have to live with what I did, knowing it was the wrong thing."[9]

Why had she gotten off relatively easily, especially for such a high-profile felony? Certainly, I believe God's mercy was at work. The judge cited her lack of a criminal record and her duties as a mother.

I finally let out a breath. So did Christine. So did our family. In tears, I hugged Christine. We thanked God for his leniency. Then a

---

9 **"I will always have to live with what I did"**: Karl Turner, "Teacher Gets Three Days in Jail for Sex with Student," Cleveland.com, June 12, 2007. https://www.cleveland.com/metro/2007/06/teacher_gets_three_days_in_jai.html.

bailiff placed Christine in handcuffs as her brief jail sentence started immediately, the consequences of her sin literally shackling her.

Then the judge decided Jagger's fate. Would we be able to raise him, even if only part of the time? Both families were committed to working together so that Jagger would have all the opportunities of a good life afforded to him. Praise God, the judge saw fit to grant shared custody.

I breathed again. The trial was over, and I prayed that all of our other trials in life would soon see resolution.

A few days after the trial, my mother sent me this prophetic word on May 12, 2006:

My Child,

Weep not my little one. I AM the God of restoration. You will see your children restored. I will bless and restore all the evil one has tried to take. Your prayers are reaching my presence, and I the Lord will act upon them.

I am doing a work in David's heart. I will use him in times ahead. Jagger is in my care, I will provide. As David seeks my face, I will guide his decision. I want him to know I have never forsaken him, but long to have him as my intimate friend. His trials will soon be over, but I am preparing a new way for him. A way not secular, but a spiritual path.

Do I not know him completely? I AM the creator, I know everything about him. Trust me, Debbie, for I have special plan for your son. He has been severely tried, but through it all, he sought my face. I know he is one of my warriors, faithful to me till the end. My word spoke life into being, can I not rescue and restore all to my children? Time for healing, time for meditating on me, and time for all things to be restored.

In the days after the trial, we believed our years-long series of trials and tribulations were also ending. We deeply thanked God for bringing us through such harrowing circumstances, for granting us mercy in our sin, and for bringing us back together as a husband and wife.

During this time, I also landed a new job overseeing global sales at MicroVision. But with all God had been teaching me over those years, I approached the job much differently. Work was no longer my priority or my identity. Rather, my job was God's provision in our lives, a way for me to support our family of five. Serving God and serving my family were my priorities. Life was returning to normal. Actually, life was returning to better than normal because we finally had our priorities right. The storms had ceased, the seas had stopped raging, and the skies seemed wide and bright.

But the calm didn't last for long. Less than two months after Christine's sentencing, the next trial of our lives arrived with the harrowing prophetic word my mother received from an angelic messenger: "Be prepared."

THE SECOND TRIAL

CHAPTER 6

A WAKING NIGHTMARE

"So Satan answered the Lord and said, 'Skin for skin!
Yes, all that a man has he will give for his life. But
stretch out Your hand now, and touch his bone and his
flesh, and he will surely curse You to Your face!'"

—JOB 2:4

How can you prepare for the unexpected? How can you ready yourself for the unknown? How can you trust God when your life is on the line?

While driving my family to church on July 7, 2007, the trees and buildings I'd so often passed by gradually turned into watercolor paintings. I wiped my eyes but found no tears or debris. I shook my head, slowed my car, and wondered what was happening to me. *Am I about to have a heart attack? Am I having one right now?* I looked at my fingers and saw more than five on each hand. Everything I saw was doubling. I shook my head again, but the world around me just became blurrier. *Something isn't right.*

I pulled over and asked Christine to drive us the rest of the way. I sat through the church service and prayed for my double vision to be healed, but the symptoms only worsened. After church, I asked Christine to drive me to the ER.

I told the doctor about my only symptom, blurry vision, and that I'd been under an incredible amount of stress in my life over the last few years. I wasn't even given a diagnosis and was promptly sent home. Knowing something was wrong, I scheduled an appointment with my regular doctor. Upon that visit, she suspected I'd picked up a virus from my travels for work. She gave me an antibiotic and told me to rest.

As far as I can remember, I'd never missed a day of work before then. But I called in sick, knowing that I couldn't perform my job while barely being able to see. I rested. I took the medication. Nothing changed. In fact, my body began turning against me. And it wasn't a slow and quiet revolution. My body had declared open war.

On Thursday, July 12, I tried to swallow one of the pills I'd been prescribed. But my throat wouldn't cooperate. It wouldn't open, not even for a sip of water. Christine saw the terror in my eyes when I realized the increasing seriousness of my situation. She rushed me back to the ER. They ran several tests to figure out my problems, but none came back conclusive.

At one point, they asked me to lay flat on my back for an MRI, but I resisted. I feared that I wouldn't be able to breathe at all in that position. They were upset, but I persisted. I was fighting for air and they weren't going to take that away from me. Later, while walking from one room to another, I collapsed. That's when the ER doctors finally realized I needed more help than they could provide. I was rushed to the Cleveland Clinic.[10]

The next morning, Friday the Thirteenth, I live a nightmare.

I can't move. I can't talk. I can't eat or drink. It's exactly like the kind of nightmare where you feel paralyzed as mortal danger steadily approaches. You scream for your body to move and it just can't. In fact, even more terrifying, when you scream, you hear nothing.

Except this is no nightmare, a frightening fact I remember every time I go in and out of consciousness. My body is quickly shutting down. I'm placed on life support. The doctors insert a feeding tube into my stomach. They force a breathing tube down my constricted throat.[11] Even though I'm not fully aware of what's happening around me, I can tell that the doctors are frantic. They don't know what to make of my condition. They run test after test and try remedy after remedy. Nothing helps. I keep declining. I wonder if I'm dying.

In the middle of that first night on life support, I wake up. No one is in the darkened ICU room except a nurse. So I pray. Well, I complain. *Lord, what's going on with me? Why are you putting me through this test? Wasn't the first test enough? Why am I going through this?* I think about all that Christine and I had just endured. Now *this*? I'm concerned about my health, but I also think about the burden I'll be on Christine and the kids. I can't bear the thought. As I'm lost in my worry, the Lord suddenly replies, "I'm with you. I'm with you every step of the way."

---

10 This would ultimately become a providential moment. Had I stayed at the ER or been transported to any other hospital, I doubt I'd be writing this book today.

11 I'd later learn that the doctors almost couldn't get the breathing tube in because I was so constricted. There was a real possibility that I wouldn't have survived that first night were it not for God looking out for me.

My soul lifts. The nightmarish clouds part, at least for a moment. God removes my fear and my pain. The terror of the night gives way to the reality of an all-powerful God calming me for the long trial I'm about to endure. "The peace of God, which surpasses all understanding" courses through my body (Philippians 4:7). I'm a disciple on a rocking boat in the middle of a disastrous storm who's just heard his savior say, "Peace, be still!" (Mark 4:39).

I'm calmed, but I know this storm isn't over. However, I also know that the wise man built his house on the rock and "the rain descended, the floods came, and the winds blew and beat on that house; and it did not fall, for it was founded on the rock" (Matthew 7:24–25). I thank God for helping to wise me up over the last few years. I believe that he is with me and will pull me through.

But my "long, dark night of the soul" is far from over.

Whatever was attacking my body was unrelenting. For every mediocre amount of progress I'd make, my body would somehow fall prey to another new ailment. At first, the doctors suspected that something had gone wrong in my blood so they ordered a blood transfusion. Then they discovered that my veins were collapsing, which meant they needed a larger tube for the transfusion. When they saw no difference in my state, they ordered a full plasma transfusion.

Pictures of me at this time show a mass of wires covering my body, electricity and technology keeping me just alive enough so that I could experience the fear of being in such a vulnerable position. But nothing worked. I felt like death and probably looked worse than that. But my heart kept beating. My lungs kept pumping. I felt like a modern-day Job and wanted to have the kind of resolute faith he had.

Even though I couldn't talk, I could at least still communicate in writing. During one of my mother's many visits, I wrote a note to her that said, "God is talking to me. He said, 'Be at peace. I will bring you through this. You are in my hands.'" But it seemed like every new day brought new suffering. For instance, the feeding tube caused internal bleeding in my stomach, which ultimately required five surgeries to fix.

On July 27, 2007, twenty days after the onset of my symptoms and a day on which I'd have stomach surgery, my mother Debbie heard the first of many prophetic words regarding my condition. Every time she received such encouragement from God, she faithfully wrote it down and shared them with me. I still have these notes today and cherish them as mementos of a mother's deep love for her son and a godly woman's abiding faith. Her prophetic words could fill a book on their own, so I'm only sharing a sampling of what she heard.

My little one,

My hand is upon your son. Trust and have faith, is this not what I have said? Surrender him, Debbie, and I your Lord will do what is best.

Yes, I have great plans for him. He has been faithful to me, and his faithfulness will be known to all generations. Take each day, surrender him to me. Fill your heart with love and positive thoughts. Be with him, and help him through this journey.

Little one, do not weep, I have heard your prayers. I AM in control, and I will be with him. Keep him in prayer and surround him with love. Love conquers all, isn't this so? Love strengthens, he has much to live for.

I will be with him today in surgery. Take care for my hand is upon him. Look up and trust the One who created him. My favor is upon him.

I love you, daughter. Have peace today.

The doctors often remarked, "I can't believe how much sedation it takes to keep you out." During one of my stomach surgeries, they learned just how much—because they hadn't given me enough. I came back to consciousness while on the operating table. I looked down at my open stomach and saw a surgeon's hands inside. They quickly put me back out.

These kinds of waking nightmares continued for the next two months. My lungs collapsed. Then I developed pneumonia. Somehow I kept existing. The feeding tube kept me nourished. The breathing tube kept me breathing. I hated them both even as I was thankful for such technology.

In the back of my foggy, sedated mind, I wondered if God had a plan for keeping me around. He gave me hope to keep enduring. But still I wondered, *Will I ever get off of this breathing machine? Will this nightmare ever end?*

On July 31, my mother shares this much-needed prophetic word with me.

"I will contend with those who contend with
you, and your children I will save."
—ISAIAH 49:25

My Son,

I see how you struggle—it is not easy to see you go through this. But I have never left your side, like a Father to his son. I will strengthen, I will guide, and in time you will see my hand. Have I ever failed you? You have always put your trust in me, even through the hardest trials.

I WILL DELIVER, I WILL RESTORE, AND I WILL USE YOU MIGHTILY IN MY KINGDOM.

Strengthen your physical body with positive thoughts, loving those most precious to you. Love does conquer, love does strengthen. Think on those you love, and love will see you through. It is the best medicine.

My son, have you not heard my voice? Comfort yourself in this, and listen for my voice. You are so precious to me, you are even engraved on my hands.

David . . . a name fitted to one who loves his God.

A month later, the doctors come into my room and ask, "Are you ready, Dave?"

They pull my breathing tube. My body finally gives up its fight. I know I'm dying.

A doctor screams, "Come back! You can beat it! Come back!" but it turns into a decaying echo. I know I'm going to be with my Lord. I recall God's Word and I hear his reassuring voice tell me, "Don't look back. Don't look back. I'll take care of the people. Don't look back. I'm taking you home."

I feel no pain, no fear. I bask in the overwhelming light of heaven. I experience the deep love, peace, hope, and joy of the presence of the Lord. I'm helpless but in the best way possible. I'm going home. My suffering is over. *If this is your will, Lord, take me.* Photos from my life, framed in mahogany, pass before me. I realize I've never seen the images before, but they're all true to my life—and they tell a condemning story. While the Lord doesn't show me the sins I've committed, he does reveal to me how much I've lived for myself. I've done nothing for his glory. My salvation is secure but my report card is empty.

As I realize this truth, the Lord speaks again. "I'm going to send you back, my son. I'm going to send you back because I have a purpose for your life."

I reply, "Whatever it is, Lord, I'll take it. I'll do whatever you want me to do."

Then the miracle-maker makes a miracle.

I close my eyes in heaven and open them in this world.

The on-call experts at the Cleveland Clinic should have gone home before I died. But, for reasons I still don't know, both the head doctor of infectious disease and the head doctor of cardiology were still at the clinic when I flatlined. The heart doctor brought me back to life, and he was the only doctor there who I believe could have done so.

In a flash, I descended from the glory of heaven to the reality of earth. I realized that I had died, gone to heaven, and met my Lord— and nothing would be the same. How could it be? God had graciously allowed me a glimpse behind the veil of this earth. He showed me without a doubt that what I had long believed to be true was absolute truth. He revealed that his Word isn't just a collection of inspirational sayings; it's reality. God exists. God loves. God judges. God has prepared a place for those who believe in him. And it truly is paradise.

When my eyes opened and I saw that I was still in the hospital and still attached to a mess of wires, I felt fearless. The world could throw anything at me now. Worrying about my career seemed like a trifling issue. Worrying about *anything* seemed minor. The worst the world could do to me was kill me—and then I'd be at home with my Lord. Yet even as I had that thought, I vowed to make the rest of my life wholly different from what had preceded it. *The next time I go home, it'll be with a full report card. Those pictures will be full of works for God's purpose—for his glory.*

Not my will, Lord.

Not my will but yours be done.

My near-death experiences aligned with what Todd Burpo shared about his young son Colton in *Heaven Is for Real*. For instance, as Todd is still coming to understand just what his son had experienced, Todd writes,

> I'd been toying with the idea that maybe Colton had had some sort of divine visitation. Maybe Jesus and the angels had appeared to him in the hospital. I'd heard of similar phenomena many times when people were as near death as Colton had been. Now it was dawning on me that not only was my son saying he had left his body; he was saying he had left the hospital!
>
> "You were in heaven?" I managed to ask.
>
> "Well, yeah, Dad," he said, as if that fact should have been perfectly obvious.[12]

12 **"maybe Colton had had some sort of divine visitation":** Todd Burpo, *Heaven is for Real: A Little Boy's Astounding Story of His Trip to Heaven and Back* (Thomas Nelson), 63–64.

As Todd asks his three-year-old son for more information, Colton describes Jesus using simple words that convey deep truths:

- "Markers, Daddy . . . Jesus has markers."
- "And he has brown hair and he has hair on his face."
- "His eyes are so pretty!"
- "He had purple on."
- "He had this gold thing on his head."[13]

Todd, who's a pastor, understood the descriptions of the beard, the eyes, the purple, and the gold. But what did Colton mean by markers? So Todd asked Colton, "Where are Jesus' markers?"

And this young child who'd never seen a crucifix pointed to his own palms and his feet.[14]

In the book's final chapter, family friends send Todd a news story about another young child who'd visited heaven and seen Jesus. Except this child, Akiane Kramarik, was a visual artist and had painted what she'd seen. In the news segment, Akiane says that "all the colors [of heaven] were out of this world." She repeats a phrase Colton had used: "He's very masculine, really strong and big. And his eyes are just beautiful."[15]

Throughout the book, Todd consistently quizzes Colton on what Jesus looked like nearly every time they see a depiction of Jesus. Colton says no every time and tells his dad specifically why any picture of Jesus isn't correct. Todd asks Colton to view Akiane's painting and asks, "What's wrong with this one, Colton?"

Colton, then seven years old, simply replies, "Dad, that one's right."[16]

13 **"Jesus has markers"**: Burpo, 65.
14 **pointed to his own palms and his feet**: Burpo, 67.
15 **"his eyes are just beautiful"**: Burpo, 142–143.
16 **"Dad, that one's right"**: Burpo, 145.

Colton was right. Akiane was right.
That's the Jesus I saw too.

CHAPTER 7

THE MEAT OF THE MATTER

"Eat whatever is sold in the meat market, asking no questions for conscience' sake; for 'the earth is the Lord's, and all its fullness.'"
—1 CORINTHIANS 10:25–26

My mother Debbie always told me, "Never underestimate the power of prayer." Surprising no one, she steadfastly prayed for my family and me throughout my lengthy hospital stay. In fact, God used one particular prayer gathering to reveal the earthly source of all my physical suffering.

After my first near-death experience, she returned home to Michigan for a barn sale hosted by the Carpenter's Daughters, a group of Christian women she belonged to who gave part of their sales proceeds to different ministries. While she wasn't working at that particular sale, she wanted to put up a sign requesting prayer for me. After all, past events had brought in more than two hundred people, and she believed I could use as much prayer as possible.

While at the sale, a friend of hers who was familiar with my long and intense hospital battle said she'd recently read an article that listed symptoms that were eerily close to mine. My mother nodded but thought little about it—until the friend's husband shoved the article into my mother's hand. Another woman at the sale witnessed that moment and said it felt like time had stopped.

My mother read the article, and I have to imagine that her eyes got wider and wider the more she read. Every symptom matched mine: double vision, trouble swallowing, trouble breathing, nausea, paralysis.

She ran into her house and called my wife. As soon as Christine picked up, Debbie asked, "Did Dave eat any chili sauce before he got sick?"

Christine paused, shocked by the strangeness of the question. But she quickly answered, "Yes. The other can is still in the cupboard."

Debbie replied, "Christine, I think we have an answer to what caused Dave's problems. I need you to go to the Cleveland Clinic right now and tell them it could be botulism from bad chili."

You may be more familiar with botulism for its most popular use: Botox. Instead of nearly killing people through slow and painful suffering, small doses of the botulinum toxin are injected into faces to remove wrinkles. Because the deadly toxin blocks nerve signals, an injected muscle doesn't receive a signal from the brain to contract.[17] Consequently, wrinkles relax. All it requires is a little deadly poison

17 **Because the deadly toxin blocks nerve signals:** "What is botulinum toxin type A?," American Society of Plastic Surgeons, 2019, https://www.plasticsurgery.org/cosmetic-procedures/botulinum-toxin.

in the right places. However, Botox is FDA-approved because the botulinum doses in it are too small to cause disease.[18]

Unfortunately, my catastrophic health issues hadn't stemmed from cosmetic surgery gone wrong. Rather, I'd contracted botulism from a can of bad chili. While that's incredibly rare, the way I'd gotten foodborne botulism was common: "Foodborne botulism occurs after the consumption of botulism toxin in foods that have not been processed correctly. This most commonly occurs after ingestion of home-canned foods, as incorrect canning procedures can promote bacterial growth and proliferation."[19]

According to the Mayo Clinic, "Botulism is a rare but serious condition caused by a toxin that attacks the body's nerves."[20] And, just as I'd experienced, symptoms "typically begin 12 to 36 hours after the toxin gets into your body. But depending on how much toxin you consumed, the start of symptoms may range from a few hours to a few days."[21]

I would eventually learn that I was one of eight reported cases in the US of botulism poisoning due to eating contaminated hot dog chili sauce. From July to August of 2007, two siblings and their mother in Texas, a married couple in Indiana, and three people in Ohio—including lucky me—had all come down with botulism poisoning. Once the poisonings came to light, the company issued a voluntary

---

18 **Botox is FDA-approved:** With a disclaimer: "Botulism can occur in individuals who receive excessively high doses of botulinum toxin type A for medical or cosmetic purposes, as well as those who receive injections of unlicensed products." From: "Is Botox® Safe?" National Capital Poison Center, n.d., https://www.poison.org/articles/is-botox-safe.

19 **"Foodborne botulism occurs":** "Is Botox® Safe?" National Capital Poison Center, n.d., https://www.poison.org/articles/is-botox-safe.

20 **"Botulism is a rare but serious condition":** "Botulism - Symptoms and Causes," Mayo Clinic, July 12, 2022, https://www.mayoclinic.org/diseases-conditions/botulism/symptoms-causes/syc-20370262.

21 **"start of symptoms may range from a few hours to a few days":** "Botulism - Symptoms and Causes," https://www.mayoclinic.org/diseases-conditions/botulism/symptoms-causes/syc-20370262.

recall. However, because of the severity of the problem, the FDA investigated the company. The FDA discovered many problematic issues and ultimately determined that the company failed to maintain certain fixtures, which allowed their food products to become contaminated.

The two other Ohio cases were brought to the Cleveland Clinic as well. One died. The other was placed on a ventilator for years. The ripple effects of one company's carelessness led to the pain, suffering, or death of those who trusted that a simple can of chili wouldn't be life-threatening.

When Christine first relayed my mom's instructions to my doctors, they scoffed. "We haven't had a botulism case in seventy years!" Plus, my symptoms were so severe that they didn't think botulism could be the cause. I could move my head, my feet, and my arms, but I was otherwise paralyzed. To make matters worse, the breathing tube prevented me from speaking. To communicate, I had to shake my head or scribble something down on paper. I thought, *At least Job could just talk and tell people what was wrong with him.*

But I also realized that not being able to speak forced me to rely on the Lord much more than I ever had before. With no expense reports to complete, no employees to manage, no traveling—with absolutely nothing to do but lie in wait for God to move—I prayed. I took comfort in the God of all comfort. I thought about one positive difference that my life had compared to Job's suffering: he didn't know until much later in his story that God had been with him through every trial and tribulation (See Job 38).

But for all my insistence that botulism was the cause, the doctors just didn't take us seriously. Not knowing what to do next, Christine called my mom. Wisely, my mom asked her to print the article and hand it to the doctors. Once they read the article and saw a verbatim list of all the symptoms I'd been suffering from, they appeared a little more open to the idea that all of my suffering was the result of botulism poisoning. At the very least, their skepticism didn't prevent them from getting my blood tested. Additionally, a new, young doctor on my case had been researching botulism and agreed with our diagnosis.

They sent my blood to the Centers for Disease Control. Since botulism is also a bioterrorism agent, the CDC is one of the very few places that can investigate such cases. By this time, I'd been on life support for seven days. Most of the doctors assumed that the chances of the CDC discovering botulism were slim to none—and slim had just left the building. Fortunately, my doctors began treating me as if I'd contracted botulism, and I have the new, young doctor to thank for being resilient in the face of others' doubt to ensure that I received the care I needed.

After Christine had shared the article with me, I was fully convinced that botulism was the physical cause of all my ailments. As we waited on the blood test results, the Lord kept confirming to both my mother and me that it was indeed botulism. The Lord was always one step ahead of us, and he was showing us the path forward. Even though my faith was firm, some doubt still crept into my mind in the middle of every night.

During a particularly restless night (every night in an ICU is restless), I close my eyes and ask a bold prayer. "Lord, if I am truly hearing the voice of God almighty, I want a sign. I'm not asking for a little sign. I want a big sign. I want to see a vision of Jesus."

When I open my eyes, I see the risen Jesus at the foot of my bed.

His radiant, unmistakable face beams at me. It feels like the first time I died. Love, comfort, and peace descend upon me. I can't believe what I'm seeing but I fully believe what I'm seeing. Jesus says,

"It's OK, Dave. Here I am." I close my eyes in acknowledgment and worship. When I open them, he's gone.

But I'm different, forever changed.

Jesus does that to people.

Six weeks later, the CDC test came back positive.

I'd contracted a deadly, paralyzing disease from an otherwise innocent-looking can of chili.

What a way to go, I thought.

As I sought to understand more about how I'd found myself in such a terrible predicament, I realized something astounding. I remembered that the day I'd eaten that fateful can of toxic chili was July 7, 2007—the seventh day of the seventh month of the seventh year of the new millennium. In God's Word, seven is the number of completion. God used seven days to create the world and sent seven plagues in Exodus. Jesus spoke seven statements on the cross. Sevens appear more than seven hundred times in the Bible. In fact, more than a hundred sevens appear in the book of Revelation alone.

God always works in triple sevens.

When I saw his hand on my life in that way and understood that he was calling me to something other than a status-quo, corporate-climber life, I asked him for confirmation. *Lord, can you show me something in a vision about this call?*

God answered me two weeks later—in an email. No, the from line didn't say "God," but neither was there a reply address. It was simply a shared YouTube link to a video titled—you can't make this stuff up— The Call. The event depicted in the video was The Call, a daylong prayer-for-revival held at Titan's Stadium in Nashville, Tennessee. The video I received was precisely ten minutes long and showed the event's epic conclusion that night. Three hundred men (representative of the three hundred men God chose for Gideon in Judges 7) marched down the aisle in unison, each man holding a shofar above his head.[22] The famous bluegrass musician Ricky Skaggs is onstage holding a shofar of his own. He blows six times. On the seventh and final blowing of the shofar, every man blasts his own shofar in loud and joyful worship of God.[23]

I watched the entirety of the video. I was awed by the outpouring of worship I witnessed. But still I wondered why I'd received that video seemingly out of the blue.

Then I saw the date that the event had taken place: July 7, 2007.

You really can't make this stuff up. God had answered my plea for confirmation with an unmistakable sign. And this early confirmation would eventually lead to a deeper calling in my life, one in which Ricky Skaggs would again play a central role.

While having an answer to the origin of my disaster brought some relief, my trial was far from over. I suffered a collapsed lung, more blood clots, and more stomach bleeding. I couldn't hold anything down or go to the bathroom on my own. I couldn't drink or speak. My world was confined to a six-and-a-half-foot hospital bed and the six inches between my ears.

My multiple issues concerned the doctors, but my first near-death experience complicated matters. The trauma of nearly dying resulted in a hole in my heart. So the doctors wanted to perform

22 A shofar is a ram's horn that was often used in worship during Old Testament times.
23 As of this writing, the video is still available to watch: https://www.youtube.com/watch?v=LCoiDehvkWE

open-heart surgery. I remember thinking, *I can barely breathe, I've died, and now you want to open my heart?*

As fear of that procedure filled my mind, the Lord calmed my heart. As he'd done so often during my time in the ICU, the Lord reminded me, "I'm with you, David. I have a purpose for you and I love you. I will make you breathe again." I believe his words of peace and comfort.

The Lord confirmed what I'd heard through my mother as well. During this time, she'd been staying at our house. The Holy Spirit told her, "Get the stitching you sent them and take it to the hospital. I'm going to help your son breathe again." God was referring to a simple crocheted stitching in a frame that she'd sent to Christine and me in the midst of our marriage troubles. Only God could know how relevant her past encouragement to us would be now. The framed stitching simply read: "Breathe deep the love of God."

When she brought the stitching to me, I excitedly wrote down on a piece of paper how that simple act was confirmation of what I'd heard and what we both believed God would soon accomplish in my life. The breathing tube that had long terrorized me would soon be gone from my life for good. I have no doubts.

Eventually, my organs and stats stabilize enough to where the doctors believe they can pull my breathing tube again. Because prior experience had taught them better, all of the clinic's top doctors were in the room. Dozens of doctors, including eight specialists and the head of the department, fill the room. I see hints of fear in most of their eyes.

"We're going to pull the tube again, Dave. Are you ready?"

I think, *What's the worst that can happen? I'll die and go home to be with my Lord.* I look at the doctors and nod yes.

They pull the tube.

Every life-monitoring device goes off.

I suddenly feel deep peace.

But I also wonder, *Why are they panicking?*

CHAPTER 8

GOD OF RESPIRATION

*"The Spirit of God has made me, And the
breath of the Almighty gives me life."*

—JOB 33:4

I see the room from a bird's-eye view. I see myself lying on my hospital-bed prison, shackled by a mass of sprawling wires and tubes. I hear doctors' panicked voices shout, "Come back! Come back! You can beat this, Dave!"

Except their voices sound muted, as if I'm hearing them from afar. I'm also calm. Again, there's no pain, no suffering. Just peace. I ask the Lord, "What are they getting crazy about? What do I need to come back for? What do I need to beat this for?"

The Lord responds, "I have you in the palm of my hand. I told you you'd breathe again. Trust me, for all things work to the good for those who love God and are called according to my purpose. And you're called according to my purpose, my son."

Joy and peace flood my soul. The Father's overwhelming uncon-ditional love fills me. I don't want to leave. I don't want to go back. But the purpose that the Lord has placed in my heart compels me to return. I slowly return to my body. The muted sounds of the room suddenly return to full force. The doctors exclaim, "He's back! He's back! We got him back. He's stable."

I open my eyes and rest in the comfort of God's promise. My enemy the breathing tube may still be stuck down my throat, but God said I'd breathe again. I believe him. He's brought me this far and shown me so much. I know he has more for me to do, and I know he's true to his promises.

On August 3, my mother receives this prophetic word for herself, an encouragement to the both of us that I would one day breathe on my own again.

> *"But as for me, I watch in hope for the Lord, I wait*
> *for God my Savior; my God will hear me!"*
> —MICAH 7:7

My daughter,

I see how your heart grieves and worry has overtaken you. But daughter, are not my words truth? Stand on them. I will be with your son, and in the name of my beloved Jesus, he will be healed! Didn't Jesus say over and over to the enemy it is written?

When discouragement comes, overpower it with my Word. Lo, I AM with Dave. I will do it! You must keep your faith strong. Didn't I say positive thoughts?

Yes, my breath will make Dave breathe again—for I AM the creator of life.

I hold the keys, and my purpose will stand. Stand against the enemy, use my Word as your sword. Didn't I say all things work toward good for those who love God, and are called according to his purpose?

Be strong, Debbie. You will overcome. My hand is on Dave.

Ultimately, I spent two months in an ICU room at the Cleveland Clinic. Following my second near-death experience, my vitals were healthy enough for me to be moved to a breathing rehabilitation facility, a place where I could be slowly weaned off of the breathing tube. However, some people doubted that I'd ever breathe on my own again. If the experts at the clinic couldn't get me off of the tube, who could? But I couldn't shake how definitive God's Word had been to me. He said I'd breathe again on my own. I knew it was going to happen. I just needed to be patient.

Finally, the day came. I'd been weaned off of the feeding tube, and now they were going to attempt to remove the breathing tube. When I began breathing on my own, I couldn't believe it. I'm pretty sure no one else in the room who knew what I'd been through could believe it either. But that moment completely drained me. Since my lungs hadn't taken in a breath on their own for more than two months, just the simple act of taking a breath wiped me out.

In fact, I would soon learn just how much my muscles had atrophied, how difficult even the most rudimentary of efforts had become. I had to relearn how to eat and drink and how to go to the bathroom.

I had to relearn how to talk—something I'd never had trouble doing before the poisoning. I was essentially an infant learning how the basic functions of life all over again. I'd been helpless in the hospital bed, but this felt just as vulnerable. I still needed to rely on many people just to get through a simple day. While I was grateful for my breath, I knew the road before me was still an uphill climb.

Then a day happens I thought I'd never get to experience again: I go home.

Creed was seven months old when I came home from the ICU. When I saw him, I cried. I was so overcome with both joy and grief. I told him, "I almost missed you growing up! I almost missed it because God almost took me home—twice!" We hugged, and I looked forward to gaining more strength so we could get back to doing all the things we loved to do together.

But life had other plans. Since my immune system had been compromised after my extended hospital stay, I was more susceptible to viruses. I came down with a severe flu bug. My body reverted to its previous state: I couldn't hold anything down again. I couldn't eat. I was weak. If something didn't change fast, I knew that I'd have to return to the Cleveland Clinic. After a few days of suffering from the flu, I planned to return the following morning.

But that night the full weight of all I'd endured finally descended upon me. I'd had it, and I let God know it. "Lord, I can't take it anymore. Why would you bring me back from death and bring me back home just to send me back to the ICU? This makes no sense. Why, why?"

As both my heartbeat and my sense of injustice increased, I paused. Then I asked an audacious request. "Lord, you know what? I don't want to hear any prophetic words tonight. I want to hear your audible voice. I want to hear the audible voice of the Most High God tonight. And I want this to go away, Lord. Take it. Take it from me. Enough's enough."

I felt like Job complaining to God: "For my sighing comes before I eat, and my groanings pour out like water. For the thing I greatly feared has come upon me, and what I dreaded has happened to me. I am not at ease, nor am I quiet; I have no rest, for trouble comes" (Job 3:24–26).

I cried myself to sleep.

At 3 a.m. on the nose, I heard someone shout, "DAVID!"

I woke up, shook the fogginess from my mind, and wondered what was going on. Then I remembered that I'd asked God for confirmation—and his love, joy, and peace washed over me. I knew without a doubt that he was confirming his voice to me and honoring my prayer. I went back to sleep, although it was fitful.

The next morning the flu was gone.

I haven't been to the ICU since.

But that's not to say my daily experience was the epitome of health. In fact, the aftereffects of botulism poisoning can sometimes be *worse* on the body than what the body experiences while on life support. Chronic pain and fatigue reign. Energy levels are less than optimal. Doing much of anything takes focus and determination. And as a man who always believed he could outwork any problem in his life, out-muscle any issue, this was a severe setback.

After being sent home from the hospital, I had high hopes that my recovery would be swift, that I could at least get back to a semblance of the kind of normalcy my life had before that fateful day I drove to church and started seeing double. But as I was recuperating at home and learning how to live and move again, I realized that God didn't want me to return to normalcy. He wanted me to return to him.

On August 5, my mom received this timely prophetic word:

"The Lord confides in those who fear him; he makes his cove-nant known to them. My eyes are ever on the Lord, for only he will release my feet from the snare."
—PSALM 25:14–15

My Son,

See my hand, it is upon you. You must begin to know my Word. My Word is life, my Word is me. As it says in Scripture, "In the beginning was the Word, and the Word was with God, and the Word was God." Do you want to know me? Then know my Word.

I have much to teach you. The Word is like a rare jewel, priceless beyond worth. I give it to you, please take it, my son, for it is wisdom.

You are not part of the world anymore, you are set apart for my glory. I will use you to glorify my name. Live each day close to me, and I will guide you.

Relationship needs time together. Is this not so my son? Time to heal, time to listen, time to know who I AM. When your time is over, only what you do for me will be of any value.

Remember my two greatest commands. Love the Lord your God with all your heart, your soul, and mind, and love your neighbor as yourself. All my law is wrapped up in love.

While God didn't poison me, I believe he allowed it to happen in order to slow me down. Even after the intense battle for my marriage, I still hadn't learned how to slow down to hear God's still, small voice. I still wanted to work hard and show my success to the world. But when you're kept alive by machines, barely hanging on to life, unable to breathe or eat on your own, you can either turn to hopeless desperation or toward the hope of the cross. With no ability to save myself—let alone do much of anything for myself—I was forced to focus on God.

And God blessed my meek faithfulness in that time. He didn't want me to rush back into corporate America just to rinse and repeat the mistakes of my past. Rather, he wanted to deeply instill in me a passion and a purpose for his glory above anything else in my life.

During that time, I thought about the apostle Paul's words in 2 Corinthians 12:7: "And lest I should be exalted above measure by the abundance of the revelations, a thorn in the flesh was given to me, a messenger of Satan to buffet me, lest I be exalted above measure." While we don't know for sure what Paul's "thorn" was, I felt as if my bout with botulism and its lifelong ramifications were my "thorn in the flesh," the weakness of my body always keeping me close to the One I need most.

Paul pleads with the Lord three times to remove the thorn. Memorably, the Lord lovingly replies, "My grace is sufficient for you, for My strength is made perfect in weakness" (v. 9a). And Paul then attests, "Therefore most gladly I will rather boast in my infirmities, that the power of Christ may rest upon me" (v. 9b).

The long trial of my hospital stay is my boast of my infirmities. "Therefore I take pleasure in infirmities, in reproaches, in needs, in persecutions, in distresses, for Christ's sake. For when I am weak, then I am strong" (v. 10).

Ultimately, I spent six months in the hospital. I died twice. I experienced heaven and saw Jesus. I heard God's voice as clear as a bright summer day. For his glory, he changed me. But it would be a couple of years before I knew just how deep that change would be.

If you had told high school Dave or Marine Dave or corporate-climber Dave that he would one day become a minister, those men may have laughed at you. But for as much as God had brought me through in the last couple of years—a marriage that should have died, a body that *did* die—I was ready and willing to believe God at his word.

Throughout August, my mother Debbie kept receiving prophetic words that were effectively God calling me to ministry. Promises like these kept reappearing:

- "Healing is coming, and you will be restored, but a new man you will be. A man of Spirit, not a man of the world. What a difference you will make when you walk in the Spirit and are obedient to my Word."

- "My son, have you not heard what I have in store for those who love me? You are one of these. A man after my own heart, as David was. My eyes go to and fro over the Earth looking for those who are devoted to me. You are one of these, my son. Oh, what the Lord can do with one soul that loves me with all of their heart. You will see the greatness of the Lord as you trust me with every detail of your life. Wilderness time is where I teach, and I will surely use you in days ahead."

- "David, do you not know I have put a purpose in your life, a purpose that will fulfill my plans. For my plans will come about for I AM the LORD ALMIGHTY. My hand is upon you son. Truth and faith are essential at this time. Do not let the enemy bring you discouragement. He knows you are highly favored of the Lord. Stand firm on my promises—they are truth."

- "Yes, I have a purpose ... which you will know in time. I surround you daily with my presence. You are ever close to my heart. Healing is coming, each day stronger, each day closer to my divine plan."
- "You are one of my warriors, so you must put up your shield against the enemy. He knows the plans I have for you. Pray for a hedge of protection each day. ... You have a heart that loves your God, and your love of me will reach many."
- "You are beloved David, by me, and by others. Use this love in a positive way—reach others for me so that they can experience this love."

I don't share these words to boast in myself. I share them to boast in my weaknesses and in God's unmistakable calling.

Throughout my many trials in the hospital, my mother continually reminded me that God uses those who trust in him while in the fiery furnaces of life. She was referencing the well-known story of Shadrach, Meschach, and Abed-Nego, the three friends of Daniel who stood up to King Nebuchadnezzar. When threatened with a tortuous death in a blazing furnace, these men of God boldly proclaimed, "Our God whom we serve is able to deliver us from the burning fiery furnace, and He will deliver us from your hand, O king" (Daniel 3:17). The proud king decides to kill them. The men are bound and thrown into the furnace. Yet the king is astonished to see *four* men within the furnace, one of whom "is like the Son of God" (v. 25). The king calls Shadrach, Meschach, and Abed-Nego out of the furnace. They walk out unscathed—but I have to imagine that their faith is more on fire than it's ever been before. After all, they've seen Jesus.

Their faith has endured the refiner's fire. No longer is it just belief; it's fact. God truly is in control of all. No weapon forged against the people of God will prosper. Not a blazing furnace or a microscopic bacterium.

To remind myself of that fact, I conduct a ritual every year on July 7: I eat a chili dog.

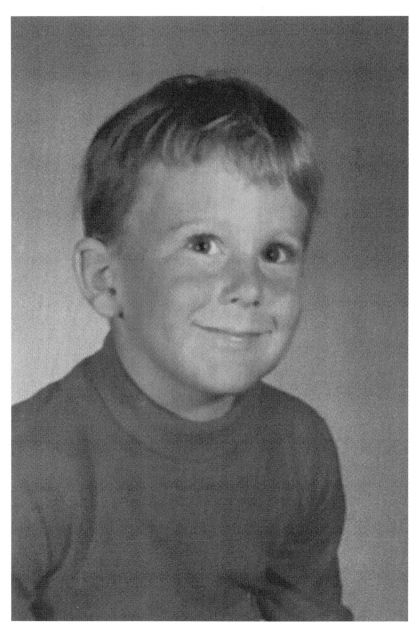

Me in the second grade

Marine Corps Ball

Marine Corps Ball

With roommate I.J.

High School Graduation

Our first Christmas together

Jagger's first Christmas

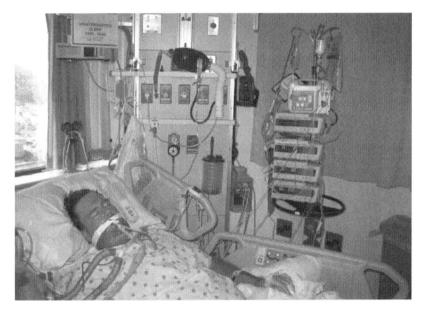

ICU 2007

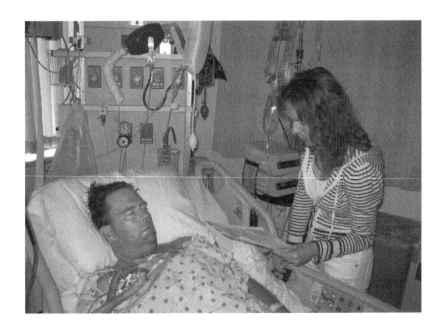

Celebrating Brittney & Jagger's birthdays in my hospital room in 2007

On stage with Ricky Skaggs

A woman asks Creed and I to pray over her

Creed and I with Orlando Magic's Johnathan Isaac

My Mom and Christine with General Flynn

Christine and I interviewing Eric Trump in 2022

Christine and I at Mar-a-Lago in 2022

THE THIRD TRIAL

CHAPTER 9

TRAINING FOR BATTLE

"Therefore take up the whole armor of God, that you may be able to withstand in the evil day, and having done all, to stand. Stand therefore, having girded your waist with truth, having put on the breastplate of righteousness, and having shod your feet with the preparation of the gospel of peace; above all, taking the shield of faith with which you will be able to quench all the fiery darts of the wicked one. And take the helmet of salvation, and the sword of the Spirit, which is the word of God; praying always with all prayer and supplication in the Spirit, being watchful to this end with all perseverance and supplication for all the saints."

—EPHESIANS 6:13–18

During my at-home recovery, I continued researching the after-effects of botulism poisoning. I read a case study in which researchers had discovered a link between time spent on a respirator and recovery. The longer that a breathing tube had been stuck down your throat, the longer your recovery would likely be. Lucky me. Actually, in looking back on this recovery period of my life, I *was* lucky because I had nothing else to do but study the Word and grow close to God.

I'd tried to go back to work but it became quickly apparent to me and everyone else that I physically couldn't handle it. I was soon placed on disability leave. Even though the Marine in me couldn't stand the idleness of not working, my body simply couldn't do much. The spirit was willing but my flesh was still very weak.

Chronic pain and severe fatigue plagued my days. In fact, I couldn't stand on my own two feet for longer than seven to eight minutes at a time. But I also knew that I needed to move regularly in order to rebuild the muscles that had atrophied so much during my extensive time in the hospital. So I set up study stations all over my house. Every station had a Bible within arm's length. Every thirty minutes or so, I'd hobble from one station to the next, pick up a Bible, and soak in the truth of God's Word. It felt a little like wandering in the wilderness and seeking God in my weakness—except the boundaries of my wilderness were only a couple thousand square feet.

I'd read God's Word every day throughout the day. Sometimes I'd listen to it on tape (remember those?). Sometimes I'd watch Bible teachers proclaim God's truth online. God taught me so much in this time that would ultimately prove to be the foundation for our ministry at His Glory. If he hadn't allowed the long trial of my hospital stay to occur, I wouldn't have had the time or energy to devote myself so fully to studying the Bible and etching his teachings into my memory. Even though I felt like I was wandering in the wilderness of my life, not entirely sure where I would wind up once I was healthy enough to resume work, I reveled in the fact that God was growing me and that I was growing closer to him.

Ironically, the wilderness period when I was at my weakest reminded me of my wilderness period when I was at my strongest. In both instances, I was being trained to fight but against two wholly different enemies.

In 1986, when I was all of eighteen years old, I joined the Marines. It was one of the best decisions of my early life. Of all the armed forces, I chose the Marines for two reasons:

- Many people see the Marines as the toughest branch and the hardest to endure. A lot of people didn't believe I could become and remain a Marine. I wanted to prove them wrong.
- I also wanted to follow in the footsteps of my grandfather, Lieutenant Colonel Kenneth Chamberlain. You may recall from an earlier chapter that he was a decorated war hero as a fighter pilot in World War II and the Korean War with a squadron known as The Death Rattlers.

I'd heard all the stories from friends and family about how difficult being a Marine would be. I acknowledged their doubts, but as a prideful eighteen-year-old I was pretty sure of my strength, both physically and mentally.

And then I went to boot camp.

Every night I'd pray, "God, just get me through tomorrow." I couldn't believe how hard the work actually was and how much of a toll it takes on your mental and emotional stamina. The day-in, day-out relentless nature of boot camp wore me down—just as it's supposed to. I'd tell myself over and over, "Just keep going. One foot in front of the other. One more mile to run, one more rope to climb." As much as I could, I focused on just the next step I had to take and not the months ahead of me with the same brutal schedule.

But one issue I couldn't help whining about was the food. The fact that we had to eat essentially the same tasteless food for weeks on end bothered me to no end. No, I never said anything out of turn to a drill instructor, but I must have complained about it too much to my family. At one point, my grandmother sent me a rich, chocolate sheet cake. While she did that out of the goodness of her heart, she should have known better. I have to think that, as a military wife, she should have known about what could happen when a private at boot camp gets a tasty treat from home.

Just as I was savoring the first bites, the drill instructor walked in. He looked at me, my fork in my mouth, and smirked. "Private Scarlett!" he yelled. "It doesn't look like you're sharing any of that cake."

I didn't reply. The mess hall went silent.

That didn't stop the drill instructor. "So I guess you'll be eating all of it by yourself. Right now."

Like a scene from nearly any movie portraying the rigors of boot camp, I dutifully yet fearfully ate the rest of my cake. Then the drill instructor made me get up and head outside, where he ran me through some of the most merciless exercises known to man. I wasn't allowed to stop until every last bit of that rich chocolate cake had made a forceful exit through my throat. The drill instructor, satisfied with his "training," then forced me to clean up the mess.

Of all the difficulties I'd faced in boot camp, that instance was particularly memorable for how it had made me feel. I felt very close to my breaking point and wondered if I'd made the right decision. But I was also so close to completing boot camp that I recommitted myself to finishing no matter what I had to endure. Plus, our Christmas break was coming up. I knew I'd get to see my friends and family soon.

However, there was one small problem: I had to pass my final test at boot camp, a rifle range test. If I didn't pass, I'd have to redo training. I couldn't imagine having to go through *more* months of the same exercises, the same food, the same mocking drill instructor. As I took the test, thoughts like that kept entering my mind, increasing my anxiety. And an anxious shooter is not a straight shooter. With every errant shot, I saw the drill instructor write something down by my name on his clipboard. I knew that it meant I was close to failing.

I had one more chance the next day. I slept fitfully. No way could I repeat training. To pass, I had to hit every target from a thousand meters away. I prayed, "Please, God, just let me hit the targets so I can go home."

I heard a still, small voice in reply: "Let go and let God."

So I did.

I exhaled, squeezed the trigger, and left the results to God. Every bullet found every bullseye. I looked on in awe. The drill instructors looked on in amazement. I don't know who was more shocked.

I passed the test and went home for Christmas.

I declined the chocolate cake.

After graduating from boot camp, I was deployed to Atsugi, Japan, as a lance corporal with the prestigious 7th Naval Fleet. I worked within a platoon of security forces that included Navy Seals. At this time, the US was on the brink of war with Iran. Our communication station was a central hub.

My duties included the reception and communication of top-secret "red-alert" intelligence. I watched with fascination as my commander dissolved written intel into a batch of chemicals after it had been read. I thought, *That information is so important to our security that we have to destroy it so it can't fall into enemy hands*. I knew what we were doing was important, but it wasn't until that moment that I truly realized the severity and necessity of our assignment.

I was grateful then and remain deeply grateful today for my time in service with the Marines. I made lifelong friends there, and some of those relationships would become crucial in my calling to the ministry and starting His Glory.

Looking back, I can see today how God used my time in the Marines to prepare me for the ministry work I'm doing now. The Marines instilled discipline in me, as well as mental and physical fortitude. Little did I know then how much I would need to exercise those characteristics in the trials and tribulations of my life. But God knew. He knew that I would one day face marriage troubles far from the norm. He knew that I would have to fight for my life. And he knew that he was calling me to "intel work" of a different sort, one that would lead to the formation of a worldwide ministry called His Glory.

But I would have to endure a different kind of training before I was ready to fully follow God's calling on my life.

CHAPTER 10

HEARING THE CALL

"There are many plans in a man's heart, Nevertheless
the Lord's counsel—that will stand."

—PROVERBS 19:21

As 2008 turned to 2009, I was still battling my health. The bad days more often outnumbered the good. My weight ballooned. My blood pressure was far too high. My skin was easily irritated[24]. I couldn't keep track of the number of medications I was on, all for the sake of trying to get me back to something resembling health and consistency in my life.

In fact, the doctors had discovered a hole in my heart during my lengthy hospital stay. But because of how physically debilitated I was, they couldn't perform surgery without risking my life. Due to the hole—and the whole ordeal of having been poisoned—the doctors

---

24 This after-effect of the poisoning still chafes me today. If you wonder why I tend to wear lounge pants in public so often, now you know!

had warned me that I'd be on pharmaceutical drugs for the rest of my life, as if it were an inevitability that the only way I could have some semblance of health was to rely on drugs devised by man.

While struggling to recover at home, I often wondered, *How much longer, Lord? If this is my normal for the rest of my life, how am I going to work? What am I going to do to provide for my family if I can barely get around?*

By God's providence, he led me to a Christian holistic physician who would prove key to my recovery. She helped wean me off of the many medications I was taking. She course-corrected my unhealthy diet. And she introduced me to essential vitamins and CBD oils. My weight and blood pressure came down. I was grateful for God's timing and his provision, and I was glad to experience the truth that God has a natural plant for all illnesses and ailments we may suffer from. I felt the effects of true healing and began to dream and pray about what God had in store for me next.

Then the opportunity of a lifetime arose.

I took my mom, Debbie, to Israel in November of 2009. I was finally healthy enough for such a long trip, and I couldn't wait to go. I'd met Jesus and seen his face. Now I'd get to see and experience his earthly home. And with as much as God had been teaching me in his Word during my recovery, I was excited to put visuals to what I'd only been able to imagine before.

Every visit to Israel is special, but the first visit is always the most awe-inspiring. To walk where Jesus walked. To see the places where he performed miracles we still read about two thousand years later. To realize the truth of all that God has done for us—that it really happened on earth, in Israel, for our good and for his glory. Your first trip to Israel will overwhelm you with history and facts and *walking*, but it will also overwhelm you with God's love, both for his people in Israel and for you personally as his son or daughter. Words can't justly describe the experience. I *implore* you to make such a trip at least once in your lifetime. You will be changed.

I'll forever cherish my first trip to the Holy Land. I immediately felt a spiritual connection to the country, an almost unspeakable kinship. I was also grateful that my mother was there with me to see the Bible come alive. In fact, the night after we arrived back home, she received a prophetic word from the Lord about me. In so many words, the Lord told my mother, "David hasn't been taking me seriously enough. For the next phase in his life, he needs to dedicate more time to learning my Word."

Inspired by the trip and challenged by God's prophetic word to my mother, I obeyed. I dedicated my days to devouring Scripture. I watched teachings from pastors like Chuck Missler, Perry Stone, Dr. Grant Jefferies, and Dr. Warren Wiersbe out of Moody Bible College, who'd done phenomenal work on the patterns of the prophets.

I did this for three years until the Lord stopped me in my tracks.

A prophetic word to Debbie on November 23, 2011:

My child,

You are listening to my Spirit. Yes, you must dig deep in the Word. My truth I will impress on your heart. I know the plans I have for you, not for evil, but to give you a hope and a future.

Humility is a must before I send you out. Pride comes in insidious ways—subtly, the enemy looks for the *weak* areas.

I know it is difficult to rid yourself of self—but the Holy Spirit will help you with this. I will lead, and you will be able to hear my voice. I ask for obedience, and I will bless you mightily for it.

You and Dave will be my mouthpieces as prophets of old. You will be grounded in my truth, even exposing my shepherds who lead my people astray. My anointing will fall and the Holy Spirit will lead you in all things.

Am I not the Lord Most High? Watch and see what I will bring to your family because of your constant prayer. It has filled the censor bowls and now I will *ACT*!

In all this, humility first, self last, that MY NAME WILL BE GLORIFIED IN ALL THINGS.

"David, you're going to start a ministry."

I couldn't believe what I was hearing. "Me, Lord?"

I wanted to laugh like Sarah laughed when Abraham told her she'd have a child in her old age. The prospect of me becoming a pastor seemed just as far-fetched. But I couldn't deny the call.

And in looking over what I'd endured, I understood that the Lord had brought me through it all in order to prepare me for such a time as this. He'd strengthened my marriage despite it almost having been shattered. He'd strengthened me despite having died. And he'd strengthened my faith by removing the idol of work from my life so that I could focus on him and him alone.

In every chapter of the story of my life, he'd been writing me toward an inevitable conclusion: a pastor for his glory.

I had no idea where to start. Did the classifieds have listings for abandoned churches? I asked God, "Do you want me to buy a church?"

He distinctly replied, "I have too many empty churches with no Spirit."

I thought about the typical road pastors take toward pastoring and began researching seminaries. I considered two of the most prestigious: Moody Bible Institute and Dallas Theological Seminary. I prayed about which one God would have me attend, but he closed those doors quickly. As I kept praying for the right instructor to lead me in how to lead a ministry, the Lord said, "I will teach you, my son."

I believed him at his word and then dove in even more into his Word. During this intense time of study, anywhere from four to ten hours per day, the Lord kept impressing upon me that my ministry would teach the gospel to the world. In fact, it would be a church on the internet. At the time, I had no idea what it would take to accomplish that. But still I trusted.

I prayed and studied as hard as a Marine training at boot camp. Except this time no drill instructor was mocking me. Rather than tearing me down, my new instructor was building me up. The Lord was restoring me, both spiritually and physically. I felt stronger than I had in years. My stamina increased. I knew the Lord was giving me just what I needed in order to accomplish what he was calling me to: a deployment to the world.

The war for souls was raging and I was being commissioned to serve my highest commanding officer.

My mission?

To spread the gospel from east to west and north to south to save a billion souls.

All for his glory.

CHAPTER 11

OBEYING THE CALL

"He Himself [Jesus] gave some to be apostles, some prophets, some evangelists, and some pastors and teachers, for the equipping of the saints for the work of ministry, for the edifying of the body of Christ, till we all come to the unity of the faith and of the knowledge of the Son of God."

—EPHESIANS 4:11–13

On September 10, 2012, the day before an Islamic militant group attacked US government facilities in Benghazi, Libya, the Lord gave me an unmistakable open vision of that very event. What I saw held true to that terrible act of terrorism that claimed the lives of two Americans, and it still holds true today. That unforgettable vision would guide much of the work we'd ultimately accomplish at His Glory.

The day began like any other. I drove my Gator utility vehicle to the front of our property in Ohio to do what I did toward the beginning of every fall season: to see how well Old Glory looked flying in the breeze. I wanted to ensure that our American flag was in good condition in order to withstand the coming winter. On that particular morning, the flag looked pristine.

Six hours later, I looked up at the flag again and noticed a glaring difference. It had been ripped nearly completely down the middle. I looked down at the Gator's display and saw 777, then the Lord too me into an open vision.

What I saw looked as if I were watching a live news report on Fox News or Al Jazeera. Riots in Middle Eastern streets. Americans under duress. Buildings on fire. I saw a man whom I wouldn't recognize until his death was reported after the terrorist act in Benghazi: J. Christopher Stevens, the US Ambassador to Libya. The vision the Lord gave me sadly played out in real time the following day.

The Lord also said, "I'm going to tear America in two. There will be division. There will be chaos. There will be attacks on the flag." As he said that, I looked up again at the cut flag flying high. I lowered it for a closer inspection. The flag seemed as if someone had taken scissors to it and cut it perfectly. But that was impossible. It wasn't windy at that time, and no one had taken it down and put it back up again. Plus, the flag had been in perfect condition just hours earlier.

The Lord also led me to understand that he wasn't just showing me events that would soon happen. He was also preparing me for what our ministry would fight against in the coming years, even into today. Islamic attacks and extremism in America weren't going to stop. Campuses would protest and riot. America would become divided.

As the formation of His Glory faced its own trials and tribulations, I knew that our country was facing even graver dangers. And I prayed that he might use our ministry to help combat those problems.

A prophetic word to Debbie on December 13, 2012:

My child,

Listen to my heart and I shall guide you. There is a great battle brewing, but you already know who has the victory. You are my warrior, stand on Scripture, it is your sword. It is truth, the light against darkness. I already paid the price. Use my WORD as your death-blowing weapon.

Debbie, times are becoming turbulent, but have no fear I go with thee. I am ever present and guide your way continually. Do not fret over circumstances, but TRUST the One who died for you—I can change hearts, my plans will stand. You are in the end days, not by happenstance but because I picked you for this time.

Deborah, in the last days, a mighty leader and warrior for her Lord. His Glory will prevail and know daughter my hand is on it. My timing and your ministry will arise with much power and anointing. You have given me your heart and all that you have. Now watch and see what I will do for you. A farm today, again a nation tomorrow.

Dave will become a mighty preacher in my name. He will exalt My Name in every way. Did I not name him after King David? He is beloved as I loved David. He is David in the end times. My servant who will exalt My Name and bring in many.

Don't let doubts arise as the enemy continues to attack your ministry. But know I have my hand on you and my purposes will STAND! Blessings will come about because you have loved your God. I see your heart, tender for me, my daughter.

Look up, for soon I will come for my precious bride! You are the redeemed, my jewels.

"Dave will become a mighty preacher in my name."

When my mom shared that prophetic word with me, I prayed about what it practically meant. God was calling me to lead a church, but not a brick-and-mortar church. Plus, I was to spread the gospel world-wide. How was I supposed to do that from the confines of my home?

In December of 2012, around the same time that my mother had received that word, the Holy Spirit gave me the name for the ministry. It was simple and straightforward: His Glory. As soon as the name arrived, the Lord began to move.

Out of the blue, my tax attorney called me. "Dave, have you thought about opening a nonprofit 501(c)(3)?"

"I have some, but it's not even close to tax time."

"I know, I know. It's just been on my mind that I should talk to you about this now."

By that point in my life, I'd experienced enough to know when God's timing presents itself. There was no more putting off God's direct call on my life to start a ministry.

"OK. Let's start a 501(c)(3). It'll be called His Glory."

As my tax attorney began the process to make His Glory a nonprofit entity, I searched "His Glory" online so that we could establish both our business name and our internet presence. But even this seemingly simple task would prove to be our first major roadblock. It seemed as if thousands of groups were already using this title or some form of it. Still, I was unswerving from God's undeniable voice that this ministry would be called His Glory. I asked for God's help in securing the name. A few days later, the person who owned the business name His Glory LLC dropped their rights to it.

Miracle number one.

I knew that we also needed to secure rights to His Glory-named websites. God told me to get HisGlory.me. At the time, I hadn't even heard of a website ending in .me. Yet again, God worked in our favor when HisGlory.me became available to us. In fact, having a .me website address helped us in the eyes of the IRS as we needed both LLC and nonprofit entities.

Miracles number two and three.

Two years after we'd launched HisGlory.me, God told me, "Get HisGlory.tv." That wasn't available, so I searched for HisGlory.tv—which also wasn't available. So I searched for it five more times. After praying about it, the website address became available to us after my seventh attempt. I should have known not to give up before my seventh try.

Miracle number four—and what a miracle that's been. Today,

HisGlory.tv ties all of our ministry work together and is visited by a million people per month. God knew what he was doing when he ordained the ministry to be called His Glory. In fact, my mother had received a prophetic word many years earlier, in 2003, that the ministry would be named His Glory. The Lord then confirmed that word to me by revealing that the Hebrew word *kavod* literally means "His Glory."

We only had one more miracle to receive, and it truly would be against a pharaoh of our day: the IRS.

In 1 Peter 5:8, the apostle Peter warned us to "be sober, be vigilant; because your adversary the devil walks about like a roaring lion, seeking whom he may devour. Resist him, steadfast in the faith, knowing that the same sufferings are experienced by your brotherhood in the world."

As the Lord was forming His Glory, our adversary wanted nothing more than to devour us. I felt this in every obstacle we faced. I would experience his persecution even more so as the ministry grew, and in very real and physical ways. But as we did all the necessary paperwork to make His Glory a ministry, we often felt as if we took five steps backward for every three steps forward. Progress seemed slow, but then I'd remind myself that "my times are in Your hand; deliver me from the hand of my enemies, and from those who persecute me" (Psalm 31:15).

Nowhere was this more excruciating than in dealing with the IRS. Their stall tactics seemed unparalleled. Over thirteen months of back and forth, we received multiple calls from different agents all saying variations of the same thing: "You can't say that your ministry is built upon the infallible, literal Word of God."

But it was. And it wasn't going to be built on anything else. I didn't know how to explain to the IRS that I couldn't just devise a doctrine of my own making. As our impasse lengthened and the window to becoming a nonprofit ministry nearly closed, they asked for twenty-five pages of verification to back up our doctrine. Everything within me just wanted to mail them a Bible with a sticky note on top that said "Read this."

But I knew that wouldn't work.

Complicating matters, Christine and I had invested $5,000 by this time into forming the ministry. Since I was still on disability, we had little income. Our life savings were dwindling. I wasn't sure how much longer I could fight the IRS or how much longer we could lose money. In desperation for resolution, I prayed for God's guidance.

That night, he answered me in a prophetic dream.

Two unmistakable IRS agents sneered at me and said, "We're going to get you!"

I angrily replied, "Get me for what? I haven't done anything!"

The agents turned their backs to me and walked toward a woman, another agent. As they were whispering to each other while pointing at me, a dam broke from somewhere and a wave of immense water flooded over them. I saw the woman's face and instantly woke up.

A few days later, I was watching the news and her face reappeared. I'd never seen her before in my life, but I learned through that news story that she was an IRS director. In fact, she was making headline news because she was at the center of a plot to deny or significantly delay the process for certain tax-exempt entities—like His Glory. Many believed she'd singled out certain groups like ours in order to render them less effective in the 2012 election. Although she issued a public apology and resigned from her post, the DOJ and the FBI both investigated her. She was not referred for criminal prosecution, but evidence was found proving mismanagement.

Maybe I should have sent that Bible after all.

A prophetic word to Debbie on September 9, 2014:

Listen to me, little one.

Have I not all of time in my hand? Don't worry when, trust my timing! Is not your God capable of anything?

I know your heart, Debbie, and how much you want to serve me. Prepare yourself for you shall surely be used. I will lead and guide and your feet I will ordain.

David is preparing, and he must be ready to face the onslaught of the ministry. He is strong in me. I will anoint his preaching. Did I not save him for a purpose? That purpose shall STAND!

Continue to fill your heart and mind with my Word. And yes, teach about Bible prophecy, my daughter. Are you not gifted in teaching? I will anoint and lead you.

Debbie, I see your heart is great for me, therefore I will use you my little prophetess. You will glorify my name!

Shortly after the scandal broke, the IRS officially approved His Glory as a 501(c)(3) organization.

Miracle number five.

Because I still wasn't fully convinced about how God wanted to form our ministry, I once again asked the Lord if I should buy a church or find a building. His response was immediate: "I have too many empty churches with no spirit. Stick with the internet!" He again pressed upon my heart that we'd be a church without walls. His Glory would minister to the world—from east to west to north to south—through TV, radio, and technology.

As I thought about the sheer depth and breadth of such a calling, the Enemy bombarded me with questions and doubts: *Who are you to be a pastor? Who's going to listen to you? You didn't even go to seminary. What do you even know about the internet? Do you really expect to reach the world?*

I countered the enemy's punches with what I knew to be true. God had called me to start this ministry. He'd brought me through so much, been at my side, and let me see his glory. He said it would happen and I believed him at his word. I recalled all the moments of confirmation he'd given me, including an intercessor once telling me that the entire world would come to His Glory, not because of me, but because of God's supernatural work in the ministry.

So, after thirteen long months of our back-and-forth with the IRS, we launched His Glory on March 19, 2013, by discussing the basics of the Bible.

I began recording live Bible studies that anyone from across the globe could watch on our website. I was far from a "natural" on screen, but practice makes perfect—or, at least in my case, just a little bit better each time, I hope. In addition to teaching through the Bible, I also shared my testimony, both about our marriage trial and the trial of my poisoning—essentially everything you've read in this book. But whenever I spoke about myself, it was boasting in the Lord's goodness to me and my family. I shared my testimony with our worldwide audience so people could know that God is real. Heaven is real. Miracles still happen. And God deeply desires an intimate relationship with you.

His Glory grew because God had a plan and a purpose: to bring his hope and truth to a billion souls worldwide.

A prophetic word to Debbie on May 17, 2014:

"I have commanded my holy ones; I have summoned my warriors to carry out my wrath—those who rejoice in my triumph."
—ISAIAH 13:3

My child,

I see your tender heart and know that you and David will follow my will and do all that I ask you to do. Your heart is heavy for the lost, as mine is too. I long for those who know me not. You *must* help bring those lost in. Timing, my timing is always right.

Never fear, never doubt, my purpose for you and Dave will stand. Can I not raise up a leader in a day as a nation? I AM that I AM. Nothing is impossible for me! Yes, evil grows but soon my saints will shine like the morning star. Brilliant, on fire for your king.

Anointing is coming. Hold fast to my Word—it is your manna. You will encounter evil, but I have overcome. Greater is he who is in you than he that is in the world.

You wonder how long, Lord, till we go out? It is soon daughter. I, your Lord, open the doors of opportunity. Do not fret or worry. My plan for you will stand. Didn't I say a farm today, a nation tomorrow? Have I not prepared you both for the wilderness? I AM is training you, readying you for the battle.

Times are going to be turbulent as my coming is soon. My saints need to be prepared with their shield but mostly with the sword, my Word. My Word will NOT come back void—that is how you will defeat the enemy. Every word in Scripture is powerful. Do I not come back with the title the Living Word? Know my beloveds I AM is always with you. I shall supply all your needs. My hand of protection is upon you. What I have ordained will *stand*!

Just give me your day and obedience and my purpose will unfold. I will speak clearly to you, Debbie. Though the world mocks you, I your Lord will be so pleased with your ministry. "If the Lord is on your side, who can come against you?"

Remember all is well. I AM is in control.

CHAPTER 12

A Revelation of Heritage

"But one of the elders said to me, 'Do not weep. Behold, the
Lion of the tribe of Judah, the Root of David, has prevailed
to open the scroll and to loose its seven seals.'"

—REVELATION 5:5

At a family member's funeral around 2014, I met a family member I'd never met before. She walked up to me and said, "David, I'm from the other side of the family, your grandfather's side."

I replied with something along the lines of, "It's nice to meet you, despite the circumstances."

Her next line caught me off guard as she spoke a deep truth into my life. "I'm jealous that you're from the tribe of Judah."

If I didn't say it, I sure thought it: *You're joking.* Our family likes to kid each other. I figured she was just trying to lighten the mood. But when I looked at her face, she wasn't cracking a smile.

In my hesitation to reply, she could tell I was dumbfounded. So she continued. "Launstein, your grandfather's last name, is a Jewish name. But do you know what it means?"

I'd never thought about it. Yes, I knew it was a Jewish name, but I'd never considered what the name actually meant. Again, my silent reply revealed my answer.

"I've researched the name. It goes back to ancient Israel. Launstein means 'of the house of David' and 'the lion of the tribe of Judah.'"

I couldn't believe what I was hearing. *Is this really true?*

That's when my family member smiled, not because she was joking around but because she could tell I was deeply affected. Not only was I part Jewish, but my lineage went back to the tribe of Judah.

What a blessing—and what a responsibility.

This is yet another reason why Israel is so important to our ministry and why you often see the unmistakable blue-and-white flag of Israel in my videos. Not only do we pray for Israel because of the biblical mandate to do so (Psalm 122:6), but I also pray for them because of my heritage. In fact, the coat of arms for the Launstein name features a lion, and that's why the logo for His Glory also features a lion.

On a more personal note, realizing my Jewish heritage through the Launstein branch of my family reminded me of a deeply special time in my childhood with my paternal great-grandmother, Ora Launstein. We had a close relationship. I'd even call it supernatural. I was blessed to spend a lot of time with her, and I often felt like a kindred spirit with her. When she went to be with the Lord when I was eleven, I was distraught. I still miss her today, but I know I will see her again.

Our family knew that she and I had a close relationship, even to the point where she'd single me out as a favorite grandchild out of her seventeen. Someone once told her, "You need to stop showing David preferential treatment or else the other kids will think you favor him."

She replied, "I do."

I still smile about that today.

When she was alive, I never knew her as Ora. She was just *Grandma*. But eventually I would learn her name *and* learn the meaning of Ora: light. I thought how fitting her name was. She was a light of the tribe of Judah. My childhood memories of her are bathed in the glow of a loving grandmother (who may have loved me the most).

CHAPTER 13

CALLED TO THE NATIONS

*"Go therefore and make disciples of all the nations, baptizing them
in the name of the Father and of the Son and of the Holy Spirit,
teaching them to observe all things that I have commanded you."*

—MATTHEW 28:19–20

Two years after launching His Glory, I had the opportunity to personally witness how God was moving in the world. On October 25, 2015, I traveled to Liberia by myself to host a crusade. Our ministry had been approached by a church there to help provide for their orphans. After a year and a half of vetting, their pastor asked me to visit their church to conduct a three-day pastors' ordination. A total of sixty area pastors attended, and we ordained each one. But the revival that concluded our trip was a God-ordained moment I'll never forget.

Prior to leaving, I was unsure if I was supposed to go alone. I was unsure if I was even supposed to go. So I asked the Lord for confirmation. Yet again, he confirmed his word to me in three different ways.

First, the Lord spoke to me and said, "Yes, you are to go there and you are to go by yourself because I, the Lord, will go and fight with you. I will be with you, and I will show you signs and wonders."

My mother then received this prophetic word on October 10, 2015: "My glory shall fall on David and they will see the mighty works of the Most High. He is faithful even with things around him are still in turmoil. For that reason, he will be David of the end times. I know, Debbie, how you long to see what I do in Liberia. You will see and know and be amazed of the wonder of your God. Signs and wonders will accompany him."

And then my brother in Christ, Pastor Brian in Kenya, shared yet another prophetic word that confirmed the word my mom had received.

In all my years of Bible study, all my long hours of prayer, and in my time leading His Glory, I've learned three truths about discerning the voice of God. Satan's chief goal is to deceive you. So how can you truly know when a message is from God? When you believe you hear God's voice, ask yourself three questions:

1. Is this message based on the Bible and taken in context?
2. Does this message give glory to God?
3. Where is the confirmation?

For the first two questions, remember this: God *always* speaks through his Word. And he *always* gives glory to himself. Satan will always subvert the Bible. And Satan will never glorify Christ. For example, just recall when Satan tempted Jesus in the wilderness. Satan repeatedly quoted God's Word to Jesus but purposefully took it out of context in order to thwart God's intentions. Jesus knew his Father's words far better than to trust the serpent's slippery tongue.

Once you've determined that a message from God is both biblical and glory-giving, seek confirmation. Pray about it yourself and see if a fellow believer confirms the message.

For example, Pastor Brian didn't know I was praying about whether or not to go to Liberia, but he shared Judges 6:14 with me at the time: "Then the Lord turned to him and said, 'Go in this might of yours, and you shall save Israel from the hand of the Midianites. Have I not sent you?'" In other words, God was confirming to me, "Have I not sent you to Liberia?" Brian also shared Judges 6:16 with me: "And the Lord said to him, 'Surely I will be with you, and you shall defeat the Midianites as one man.'" This confirmed to me that I was supposed to go by myself to Liberia because surely God would be with me.

So I obeyed God's word and traveled to Liberia solo. I thank God to this day that I was obedient to his voice that year.

I was there during the rainy season. Torrential downpours occurred almost every day. On the next-to-last night of the crusade, God spread a double rainbow across the sky. A Liberian pastor in attendance told me he'd never seen a double rainbow in his lifetime. It was as if God was telling us to be ready for his outpouring. On the last night of our crusade, he would show his power.

Although the rain surrounded us, our area stayed dry, as if God were holding up the rain. The lighting wasn't strong, but God had hung a full moon above us. Its beam shined like a spotlight on the place where we were worshipping. We felt his palpable Presence.

More than seven hundred Liberians accepted Jesus Christ as their Lord and Savior.

As we prayed in the Spirit, a woman was rescued from a demonic possession.

A six-foot-six, two-hundred-and-fifty-pound man—reportedly the biggest man in all of Liberia—was slain in the Spirit five times.

This showed to all in attendance just how powerful the God of the Most High is.

And fifty people or more felt the power of the Holy Spirit and spoke in new tongues.

The rain didn't fall on us that night. Rather, the power of God poured down.

When you hear a word from God, make sure it's biblical and God-glorifying. Seek confirmation. Then agree with the prophet Isaiah and say, "Here am I! Send me" (Isaiah 6:8).

If you don't, you will miss out on untold blessings in your life.

A prophetic word to Debbie on May 23, 2016:

"Not by might nor by power, but by my spirit."
—ZECHARIAH 4:6

My daughter,

How I have longed for you, my daughter. I see your love for me and your desire to serve. I AM is with you in all that you do. I will protect, I will strengthen, I will set your feet upon a path. You will bring *glory* to My name!

Time to get your physical house in order. You must get ready for the days ahead. Exciting days as your heart will soar as you see your Lord in action. I care so much for you, Debbie. You are one that loves her God and seeks his face! You bring much joy to my heart! The joy of the Lord will be your strength. If I send you out, I will give you the strength for what I call you to do!

Soon little one you will be traveling to other countries. Healing will flow from your hands as you touch people in my name. I know you will give me all the glory, as you and David have put me first in everything you have done for this ministry. I will exalt you, supply all your needs, and will use you to bring in the harvest. A mighty outpouring is coming ... a *drenching*!

I see your joy at being with Robin Mark in worship. His heart is for me and I know you sense my presence in his worship. Did I not give you the desire of your heart, little one? Will I not fulfill the other desires? Your desires are not for you, but your desire is for me, and that touches my heart.

Hang on to your hat, get ready to go, for I AM is about to launch a great ministry. Stay focused on me and in my Word. I will supply all your needs and give you the words to speak. A mother/son ministry that glorifies my name. You will be blessed by the Most High as you go out among the nations.

His Glory nations will arise and multiply for I will do it saith the Lord.

I taught through all of the New Testament and a majority of the Old Testament. As we witnessed traction on our website and our audience grew, we expanded our ministry to use other platforms like YouTube and Facebook. This, of course, would come with its own persecutions. For instance, YouTube deplatformed us in May of 2021. All of our Bible studies, which numbered into the hundreds, were deleted. Fortunately, we had backups and were able to restore our channel, but our trust in YouTube would never be restored.

Our Facebook account was hacked multiple times as well. At one point, the hackers were pretending to be us and posting curse words to our page with 1.2 million followers. We tried to contact Facebook, but they never responded. They didn't even have a customer service line to call. After repeated attempts to get our account restored to us, I decided that we were done spending the Lord's money with that company. On November 5, 2018, I posted a video to our followers on YouTube that told them about the hack on Facebook, as well as the death threats that had been coming my way. I asked our followers to start checking our site at HisGlory.me for any new content. While the Facebook hack was frustrating, the timing was providential. We'd just announced that we were going to build a studio, and we saw God shut the door on Facebook so he could open the door to our website.

This was just one of many obstacles we faced as His Glory grew from God's calling on my life to encompass a worldwide reach. But one persecution in particular would strike far too close to home.

CHAPTER 14

PROWLING AT OUR DOOR

"Have I not commanded you? Be strong and of good
courage; do not be afraid, nor be dismayed, for the
Lord your God is with you wherever you go."

—JOSHUA 1:9

I n 2018, a stranger knocked on our door. Christine answered and
opened it. The man asked about an item that she'd recently put up
for sale on Facebook's marketplace. She could tell he was out of sorts
and acting strangely. I heard their conversation and grew concerned,
so I walked from the back of the house toward the front door. As
soon as the man saw me, he turned around and fled. Christine quickly
shut the door and locked it. We both felt uneasy about the experience but thanked God that nothing had come of it. Still, I filed a
police report just to be safe.

Days later, we saw that man on the news. According to one
article at the time, "A Maple Heights man plotted to set off a bomb

at the Fourth of July fireworks celebration in downtown Cleveland in an attempt to 'strike at the values at the very core of our nation,' authorities said." The man had "expressed a desire to join al-Qaida and kill U.S. Citizens—including military personnel and their families."[25] When Christine and I heard that news and saw that man's face on the local news, we thanked God that he'd been caught before his insidious plot came to fruition. And we were once again grateful for God's protection of our family.

Spiritually speaking, the man had chosen us because the devil was still prowling around. Earthly speaking, I believe the man had chosen us because of the growth of His Glory throughout the world. Our ministry was five years old at that point, and we were reaching more and more Muslims in the Middle East.

In fact, it was around this time that we launched *Take Five*, an interview-style show that's still our most popular series. The Lord had impressed upon my heart to combine my military experience with my biblical knowledge and to give a voice to censored patriots and Christians fighting on the front lines of the culture wars. Surprisingly—but not surprising to God—the show became popular in Muslim countries. Because of this show, two Muslim religious leaders, a.k.a. imams, gave their lives to Jesus. One imam even provided his testimony via Facebook live. I believe that Christine and I had been targeted my Muslim extremists because we were the founders of the ministry that had resulted in that imam's conversion.

It seemed that for every Muslim who responded well to God's message of hope, a dozen more would threaten us in some manner. The man who'd shown up to our house was the first Muslim extremist

25 **"expressed a desire to join al-Qaida and kill U.S. Citizens":** Adam Ferrise and Evan MacDonald, "FBI Details Suspected Fourth of July Terrorist Plot for Downtown Cleveland," Cleveland.com, July 2, 2018. https://www.cleveland.com/metro/2018/07/maple_heights_man_accused_of_p.html.

to try to fulfill those threats on our lives. He wouldn't be the last, unfortunately. But we stayed resolute in God's promise of protection.

Throughout this ordeal, we also received confirmation from the FBI that terrorist cells were operating at that time in Cleveland. Again, lucky me. I just so happened to be in a hot spot of terrorism while our worldwide ministry was striking at the very heart of their religion with the truth of God's Word. Fortunately, our local sheriff took the threats on our lives seriously. After our visit from a terrorist, patrol cars routinely drove by our house to ensure our safety. Every time I saw them making their rounds, I'd thank God yet again for his protection. His Glory was his ministry, and the wayward ways of man wouldn't stop him from making it grow.

Around this time, one of my mom's prophetic intercessors received this prophetic word:

> Dave, This is your time, your time to believe. This is your time to trust. Trust Me with all that you are and all that I have called you to be. Do you believe what you teach and what you preach? Haven't I said I would provide all your needs, haven't I called you to be My servant? Yes, hard times are part of the process for great faith. You are my son I have called you by name since before you were born. I have brought you here to this place in time to learn to trust and teach others the same.
>
> I will never leave you or forsake you. I will provide. Believe and trust Me. I know you are being stretched, but hold on tight to what you know, the Word. I know you, even when you doubt and fear, you love Me and trust Me. I am strengthening you in these hard times. I am teaching you

and you will be a witness for great faith. This is another step higher, keep on looking up; I am here. Believe!!!!! Matt 6:8 Your father knows what you need before you ask him. Praise Him for every answer before you see it.

Christine, I have called you to pray. I have gifted you for such a time as this. I see your heart. It is a pure heart. It's not the eloquence of words you pray, but the heart of love you have for Me. This is your gifting for now. Watch, I will add more. Seek but wait and be patient. I am working in you. You are strong, a tower of strength for Dave and your children. You have learned how to open the door. Never hesitate to come. I will give you rest. I love you.

CHAPTER 15

PROVIDENTIAL ENCOUNTERS

*"As iron sharpens iron, So a man sharpens
the countenance of his friend."*

—PROVERBS 27:17

God continued to open doors for our ministry to meet men and women he was using to influence the culture for his glory.

On August 5, 2019, I interviewed Dallas Jenkins for *Take Five*.[26] At the time, he wasn't that well known (aside from being the son of Jerry Jenkins, author of the famous *Left Behind* series of books). You may still not know the name Dallas Jenkins, but you likely know the name of the show he created: *The Chosen*. When we interviewed Dallas, they were wrapping up the filming of the final four episodes

---

26 **interviewed Dallas Jenkins for** Take Five: "The Chosen and Dallas Jenkins on HIS GLORY Nation Www.hisglory.me," August 5, 2019, https://www.youtube.com/watch?v=wvWFMh2wtmQ.

of their first season. Back then, the show had yet to achieve the broad popularity it has today. But the Lord had impressed it upon me to support Angel Studios and *The Chosen* back then. We would often play trailers on HisGlory.me for its first season. I believe that the increasing popularity of the show also helped us grow in popularity.

Since we were reaching more people, God laid it on my heart to start a show called *A Window into the Supernatural*. I was to highlight the prophetic, supernatural parts of Christianity that so often weren't directly discussed. Guests would share their testimonies of prophetic visions, dreams, and words, all giving us a glimpse into God's plan for our future.

On December 12, 2020, I attended the Jericho March's "Let the Church ROAR" event in Washington D.C. Along with leaders like Eric Metaxas and pastor Greg Locke, thousands of us prayed, fasted, and marched to save America and expose the election fraud that had just occurred in November. While there, I met General Michael Flynn, who'd been President Trump's National Security Advisor. I had breakfast with pastor Bryan Gibson. And I met Aaron Antis, the vice president of sales for Shaw Homes. Aaron worked closely with Clay Clark and was also a fan of our work at His Glory. He asked if he could introduce me to Clay because God had laid it upon Clay's heart to devise a plan to wake America up. In fact, Aaron told me that Clay had written a list of names to be involved on a whiteboard and Dave Scarlett was on that list. With that kind of confirmation, I knew God had ordained me to be part of what Clay and Aaron were putting together.

Months later, on the momentous day of January 6, 2021, I was in Washington D.C. with Clay Clark and thousands more patriots to support President Trump. I witnessed an unforgettable scene of so many men and women praising God and also voicing their opposition to a stolen election. It was undeniable that God was up to something big in our country. Years later, His Glory would be instrumental in releasing a documentary about this day titled *Capitol Punishment*. For a fuller recounting of what that day was truly like, I encourage you to visit our website to watch the trailer and purchase the documentary.[27]

Shortly after the events of January 6, I met with Clark and he formally invited me to take part in his first ReAwaken America tour. This would be another pivotal point, both in my life and in the ministry of His Glory, and it would include an incredible, God-ordained moment that would bring my triple-seven experience full circle.

In this same time period, three different people introduced me to the same man in just one week. Even though this man didn't know me, he'd long been an essential part of my story. Aside from enjoying his music and appreciating his public stance for God, this man had played a central role in God's call on my life. So I can't say I was surprised when those three people introduced me to Ricky Skaggs. We soon connected, and I knew it was a Holy Spirit-led encounter, the Lord putting us together for such a time as this.

We became friends. I invited him to be a guest on HisGlory.me. We spoke about the blowing of the three hundred shofars on July 7, 2007. What follows are Ricky's own words penned for this book about how he remembers that unforgettable night:

27 https://hisglory.tv/capitol-punishment/

My name is Ricky Skaggs. If you're in the ministry, you've probably never heard of me, or you might have said, "Oh, he's that guy that plays bluegrass and country music. I think he's a Christian but he goes to bars, casinos, beer joints. and does a few gospel songs."

Well, you'd be right!

There's an incredible "God Story" I'd like to tell you.

Back on July 7, 2007, (7-7-07) there was an event called *The Call Nashville*, hosted by Lou Engle and Dutch Sheets to pray, repent, and prophecy.

My friend Ray Hughes had gotten a word from the Lord to put together a Gideon's army of three hundred people who could blow the shofar and break open the heavens. He put out invitations months before, and three hundred signed up from all over the country. As a musician and a spiritual father in Nashville, Ray had asked me to lead the charge to blow seven blasts, and on number seven all the rest of the shofars would join in.

That was the loudest band I've ever played with in my life. It was also one of the most powerful experiences I've ever had. Even now watching it on video, the presence of God is still there. I cry every time I look at it. Even the stadium shook. I've seen video footage of that too.

One of the God things that happened around this particular part of the event was Ray counting the people who had signed up to blow the shofar, to make sure everyone was there and to give them instructions on how we were going to do it. We had 299 counting me. But Ray was sure about what he had heard from the Lord, "Gideon's army of three hundred!" So they counted them one more time and came up with the same number: 299. I'm not sure if Ray was giving number three hundred some more time to show up or not, but Ray did an Isaiah 22:22 expression of faith. He had everyone in the stadium take out their keys and shake them just to remind the devil that we as believers in Jesus were given the keys of the kingdom to bind and to loose things in the heavens and on earth. That went on for minutes. The whole stadium was filled with the sounds of those keys rattling. It was a powerful act of faith for seventy thousand people to realize what authority we have in the Lord Jesus.

It was getting time for Ray to lead this part of the event, so we went for it anyway. Little did we know till afterwards that the last guy showed up just in time to march up in front of the stage right before we started to blow the shofars.

He told Ray afterwards that he was really sorry he was late, he had come down to Nashville from up in the northeast, he drove all night and day to get there. He got held up in traffic! But when the Lord calls for a certain thing to be done, he will move heaven and earth—and a traffic jam or two—to get his purposes fulfilled.

After Ricky told me about his unforgettable 7-7-7, I told him what I'd been up to on that same day: just eatin' chili and wondering what God was going to do in our lives after the severe trial we'd just endured in our marriage. Of course, I also told him about everything that happened after having been poisoned. I described dying, going to heaven, and seeing photographs that revealed how my life had fallen short. I told him about seeing Jesus at the foot of my bed. I let him know about the suffering I'd endured but only to boast in my weakness that God may be seen as my strength.

Broken up, Ricky felt the Spirit of the Lord come upon him. He talked at length about The Call on July 7, saying how he'd never experienced anything like that night in his life. He felt the stadium's steel rafters shake with the reverberations of three hundred shofars. He felt the power of the Holy Spirit like he'd never felt before.

Knowing that God had brought about our friendship for a reason, I asked Ricky to be my personal guest at the first stop on the ReAwaken America tour. He gladly agreed.

The tour began in April as a "Health and Freedom" event to protest what was being forced on Americans during the COVID-19 scare. Our first stop was in Tulsa because, according to Clay Clark, Kenneth Hagin had once prophesied that "there would be an atheistic, communist, Marxist and racially divisive spirit that would descend upon America . . . and that the spark of the revival would start from Tulsa, Oklahoma."[28]

I was one of many speakers for the event, and I was set to take the stage with Floyd Brown, the owner and founder of the Western Journal. Before going on, we both decided not to talk about the jab or anything medical. Rather, we wanted to invite the Holy Spirit to come down from east to west and north to south and let healing begin. The Lord impressed upon me that Ricky should blow the shofar before we spoke. Ricky gladly obliged.

When I heard the distinctive blare of his horn, I couldn't help but think about the first time I'd ever heard Ricky blow a shofar, from that video on a day I'll never forget. As the sound carried over the

---

[28] **"the spark of the revival would start from Tulsa":** Marti Pieper, "Clay Clark Explains How Prophecies by Kenneth E. Hagin and Kim Clement Inspired ReAwaken America Tour and Documentary," Charisma News, December 6, 2021, https://www.charismanews.com/news/us/clay-clark-explains-how-prophecies-by-kenneth-e-hagin-and-kim-clement-inspired-reawaken-america-tour-and-documentary/.

crowd, I thought about all that the Lord had brought me through and all that he was calling me to. Once the sound of the shofar had ended, I prayed over the crowd, "Holy Spirit, come down from east to west to north to south."

The place went silent.

A thick cloud of glory descended upon us. The Holy Spirit was visiting his people, making his palpable presence known. Many were healed. Some in wheelchairs arose and walked. Some with Stage 4 cancer later told us they'd been cured. People lined up for prayer from one end of the stage to the other. They wept as they worshipped. Just as the Bible had said so long ago, signs and wonders were happening. I couldn't believe my eyes, but I always believed my God.

After God moved in his power and might during that moment, Ricky visited a backstage green room that His Glory had set up in order to interview guests of the event for our live-streaming internet audience. While I was interviewing Ricky, the Holy Spirit came over him. Ricky said, "The Lord's told me that you, David, should have this shofar." Ricky showed me the shofar that he'd just played on stage.

I smiled.

"It's the same shofar I played on July 7, 2007."

I wept.

We went back onstage, and Ricky presented the shofar to me in front of the eight thousand people in attendance. Ricky said that the shofar was for my call to His Glory.

To this day, I love to tell the story of the shofar that proudly sits in my office. It's one of my most treasured possessions, not because it was given as a gift from a friend and an impressive musician and Christian man, but because that shofar symbolizes God's perfect care and his undeniable calling on my life. I believe it was also God's way of saying, "I'm calling another Gideon out for my glory."

Thank you, Ricky, and thank you, God.

Because of the ReAwaken tour and because of His Glory's growing ministry, I've had the God-given fortune to meet so many people I never thought I'd meet, much less befriend.

For instance, I'll never forget having MyPillow founder and CEO Mike Lindell on *Take Five* for the first time. Although the enemy attempted to thwart our meeting with early technical problems, God redeemed the situation. Mike ultimately shared his full testimony of how he came to know God and what had led him to fight for America. At one point during his testimony, I thought back to 2015 and remembered my boys, Creed and Jagger, laughing at me. We'd just seen a MyPillow commercial. Out of the blue, the Holy Spirit spoke to me. Then I told my boys, "Mike and I are going to be friends one day." I can still hear their laughter. What's even more fascinating is that Creed would eventually get to interview Mike as well and also develop a friendship with this modern-day Paul Revere.

Since the ReAwaken tours were a gathering of American patriots, most of whom supported President Trump, it wasn't long before the tours gained the Trump family's attention. In fact, General Flynn introduced me to Eric Trump, and Eric eventually joined us on a few stops of the ReAwaken tour. I believe that the Trump family, and particularly Donald Trump, have been anointed by God to lead America. I was amazed at God's way of connecting our ministry to the Trump family. But I was more amazed that God had confirmed a dream he'd given me all the way back in 2008.

I was in the White House media room for an important meeting hosted by, of all people, late-night talk show host David Letterman. Seven smartly dressed men and women sat at the table next to me. Within this dream, I automatically knew that they represented the seven mountains of family, religion, education, media, arts and entertainment, business, and the government and military.[29] Letterman was cutting jokes about the news just as if he were on his show, but no one in the room was laughing. I had the distinct thought, *What if he's telling the truth?*

Although I was sitting separately from everyone else, I suddenly felt a nudge on my side. I turned around to see Vice President Dick Cheney. Remember: this dream occurred in 2008, when Bush and Cheney were still in the White House. I thought how strange that Cheney would be here. Then Cheney looked at me, pointed to Letterman, and said, "You know what he's talking about? That's a house of cards—and the whole thing is coming down. Every one of them is going to be exposed."

In the dream, I knew he was talking about 2008. The financial collapse was imminent. But I also believe this prophetic dream still holds true for today. God is going to expose the seven mountains.

My dream didn't end there though. Funnily enough, my answer to Cheney wasn't very logical, but it led to a fascinating reply. When Cheney said, "It's a house of cards," I replied, "I'm from Michigan. The only card game we know is euchre." Cheney simply said, "You're going to have to play your trump card." Then the dream ended.

I never forgot that indelible prophetic dream, but I also wondered for quite some time what Cheney meant at the end. In 2008, I wasn't aware of Trump's aspirations for the presidency. But as Trump grew in influence and was eventually elected president, I understood what the Lord had been trying to tell me in that dream. Not only was Trump going to be an important figure in American history, I also believed that God would use him to help bring down the seven mountains of influence that have been taken over by secular values.

29 If you're unfamiliar with the Seven Mountain Mandate, I discuss it more in the next chapter.

And so I am grateful still today for our ministry's connection to the Trump family, knowing that God is using him to redeem America.

All through this time, the Lord kept growing His Glory. We began interviewing more leaders from many areas of culture, from politicians to pastors, music artists to prophetic voices, movie stars to military heroes. They shared heartfelt testimonies of how God had moved mightily in their lives.

We were part of God's movement to reclaim the seven mountains of influence in America.

CHAPTER 16

THE SEVEN MOUNTAINS

"So Jesus said to them, 'Because of your unbelief; for assur-
edly, I say to you, if you have faith as a mustard seed, you
will say to this mountain, "Move from here to there," and
it will move; and nothing will be impossible for you.'"

—MATTHEW 17:20

What are the seven mountains, and why do they matter to the future of America?

These seven essential areas of influence deeply affect us now and will define what our collective future looks like. Currently, the enemy has claimed his stake and planted his flag at the pinnacle of each of these mountains.

As a Marine, I know that the first step in overcoming an enemy is to gather as much intel as you can. So I prayed about the state of our nation, and the Lord revealed to me that these seven mountains were the key to restoring America, not just for us today but also for our children and their children. The ripple effects of restoration could last generations. Remember Deuteronomy 7:9: "Know that the Lord your God, He is God, the faithful God who keeps covenant and mercy for a thousand generations with those who love Him and keep His commandments."

- In religion, we seek to revive the spiritual heartbeat of our communities.
- In education, we strive to cultivate minds grounded in truth and wisdom.
- In family, we long to strengthen the bonds that hold society together.
- In business, we want to foster a marketplace where integrity, innovation, and stewardship flourish.
- In government, we advocate for righteousness in leadership and legislation, following the Constitution that our forefathers established.
- In arts and entertainment, we seek to inspire beauty and truth through creativity.
- In media, we work to shape narratives that celebrate our values and virtues.

By focusing our efforts on these seven mountains of influence, we believe at His Glory that we can usher in a new era of godly governance and divine prosperity.

But Satan's claim to each mountain is strong.

Religion

Despite what historical revisionists would have us believe, America was founded on Judeo-Christian values. The First Amendment of our Constitution demands freedom of religion. Every state constitution mentions God. And the separation of church and state was initially provided to protect *the church* from the state and not the other way around, as our government would have us believe today. Yet secular America seems bent on erasing Christianity's influence. The examples are legion—just watch the nightly news. But I think about the military and employers refusing to acknowledge religious exemption forms when it came to the experimental COVID shot. Or public school teachers being forced to call children by their preferred pronouns. You don't have to look very hard for ways in which our government and our culture are seeking to erase Christianity.

Unfortunately, it's almost understandable. We suffer from in-fighting. Too many denominations following too much manmade doctrine leads to internal wars that lessen the impact we could have as a united front of Bible-believing Christians. This is one reason why God called me to establish His Glory on his infallible Word. Who was I to argue against God's first foundation? "In the beginning was the Word, and the Word was with God, and the Word was God" (John 1:1).

Again, the pandemic revealed much. While some lukewarm churches and their leaders conformed to their government's woke ideology, others stood strong, even putting their jobs and freedom on the line. I think of Pastor Artur Pawlowski out of Canada, a good friend who refused to conform to his country's unconstitutional ordinances. He kept his church open during the pandemic and suffered fines and incarceration as a result. But he obeyed what God had placed on his heart. In fact, his testimony led to the formation of our show *Lions and Generals*, which I cohost with Pastor Todd Coconato. Pastor Pawlowski was our first guest, and we would go on to highlight the people who weren't afraid to stand up for God and country. We need more lions and generals in our faith today. And we need to pray for the revival of the spiritual heartbeat of our communities.

Education

Christian parents—and particularly those with children in public schools—don't need the battlefield of education described to them. They experience it every school day, at parent-teacher conferences, and in tense school board meetings. They see how sexuality is promoted, how LGBTQ identification is normalized, and how it's OK to define yourself against what God created you to be. These parents have learned how secular, collegiate-level ideologies like Critical Race Theory and Marxism have trickled down into even elementary-school level teachings. For some who have spoken out against these issues, they've been labeled "domestic terrorists" for simply voicing their dissent.

The COVID pandemic was horrific for many, but I believe God used forced virtual learning to expose the mountain of education. Because parents had to become more involved in the day-to-day of their children's education, they became more aware of what their children were actually being taught. And the Christian parents who cared that their children were effectively being indoctrinated with secular, even devious, ideologies woke up and spoke up. May we strive to cultivate minds grounded in truth and wisdom.

Family

Arguably, the Christian ideal of the traditional family has been playing defense ever since the sexual revolution of the 1960s. Today, the notion of family faces an onslaught from every side. When both parents work (due to the increasing difficulty of living within our economy), children are mostly raised by their teachers, other family members, or their phones and tablets. When parents are divorced or separated, children suffer in a number of ways that tend to long outlast their childhoods. And when the definition of family is extended to include same-sex couples or even polyamorous groups, how does a traditional, biblical definition of man and woman in holy matrimony survive in our culture?

For all the detrimental toll that redefining *family* and *marriage* has taken on our culture, the most horrific attack has been on those who can't even defend themselves. I praise God that *Roe v. Wade* was overturned, but abortion rates actually increased in the year following the reversal.[30] Abortion has long been one of Satan's most devastating and most strategic attacks on the family. We must do better on behalf of the millions of children who were silenced before they ever spoke their first word. Let us work together to strengthen the bonds of family that hold society together.

Business

Many people who aren't Christians know a few Bible verses. They may not know that a certain sentence or phrase is from the Bible, but they know the words carry deep meaning. I hope that most people today would be able to complete this sentence: "The love of money is . . . ." Now, most people may say, "The root of all evil." They'd be wrong, but only barely. In Paul's letter to his protégé Timothy, Paul actually wrote that "the love of money is a root *of all kinds* of evil" (1 Timothy 6:10). And nowhere does this truth of God's Word play out more visibly than on the mountain of business. In bowing to the Almighty Dollar, our businesses oftentimes work from a position of greed instead of generosity.

And to make matters worse, the largest businesses and corporations in America tend to have an outsized influence on our culture. Just consider how many large businesses have recently adopted "woke" policies. When it comes to the mountain of business, we want

---

30 **abortion rates actually increased:** Jason Milman, "Abortions increased the year after Roe was overturned," Axios, October 24, 2023, https://www.axios.com/2023/10/24/abortion-increase-roe-wade-state-ban.

to foster a marketplace where integrity, innovation, and stewardship flourish.

Government

As you know, our government in America holds immense sway, not just in establishing, maintaining, and enforcing our laws but also in controlling the culture's future. How would God have us govern? Whom would he lead us to vote for? What issues should be our rallying cry? We advocate for righteousness in leadership and legislation, following the Constitution that our forefathers established.

Arts

The mountaintop of arts and entertainment may be the most visible area of influence that the Enemy holds. We can't escape the prevalence of TV, movies, the internet, video games, or any of the dozens of other ways that we're entertained these days. But a vast majority of this "entertainment" isn't meant to edify, and it's certainly not being created to spiritually edify. While strides have been made to create better, more compelling Christian content on various media venues (e.g., *The Chosen*), much of what we see on screens teaches the ways of the world. And the fact that such entertainment can reach millions across the world should give us pause. In arts and entertainment, we seek to inspire beauty and truth through creativity. By creating alternative narratives that honor God (instead of honoring sin), we believe we can transform culture through the very same lenses that the Enemy has such a stronghold on.

Media

Finally, the media may be more of an extension of entertainment now more than ever. What can we truly believe about what we see reported on our screens? How can we not take into consideration the slanted viewpoints often presented as the only truth of a news story? Where can we turn for God's take on what's happening? When it comes to the mountain of media, we work to shape narratives that celebrate our values and virtues.

All of our work at His Glory aims to topple the influence of the Evil One over each of these seven mountains. We've had the blessing to speak to so many people who are on the front lines of these issues, and I encourage you to visit HisGlory.me to hear more from them.

The task may be large. It may even be insurmountable, but that's speaking in human terms. Take courage from Jesus's words in Matthew 17:20: "If you have faith as a mustard seed, you will say to this mountain, 'Move from here to there,' and it will move; and nothing will be impossible for you."

What will you say to these mountains?

CHAPTER 17

HIS GLORY TODAY

"Therefore take up the whole armor of God, that you may be able to withstand in the evil day, and having done all, to stand."
—EPHESIANS 6:13

In seeking to reclaim each mountain of influence, His Glory works to expose lies, share truth, and spread the gospel. We strive to live up to our calling, and we weren't called to be still.

God kept weighing on my heart to refute the lies the media had been telling about January 6. I prayed about my unrest. Three times in one week, different people told me to meet actor and director Nick Searcy. Around the same time, my friend Floyd Brown had been seeking financing for a documentary about the truth of January 6, but he couldn't land the money he needed. That's where God called me into that work. Despite the fact that His Glory didn't have additional finances to help with that project, I knew I had to be obedient to

God's call. We released *Capitol Punishment* on November 25, 2021. It continues to be the most censored movie ever.

A year later, our ministry would take on a similar role in bringing the truth to light about the horrors of human trafficking on our southern border. Along with a video team, I traveled to Arizona and met Sheriff Mark Lamb. We captured footage of what was really happening at our open border. I saw grown men with children with no way of knowing if they were related or if something far more nefarious was occurring. In addition to increased human trafficking, drugs were pouring through our porous border. Murders were high. Lawlessness seemed to be the law of the land. And yet the administration did nothing. We felt led to expose the truth in another documentary titled *Beyond the Border*.[31]

As God leads us, we will continue to seek ways to leverage our reach and our God-given talents to bring light to the stories that mass media doesn't want the world to know about.

Unfortunately, there's always a price to pay for standing up for the truth, and I've personally learned that in a number of troubling ways.

Whenever I think about the suffering that Christians the world over endure because of what we believe, I take courage from God's Word, and particularly from what Jesus said in John 15:18–20: "If the world hates you, you know that it hated Me before it hated you. If you were of the world, the world would love its own. Yet because you are not of the world, but I chose you out of the world, therefore the world hates you. Remember the word that I said to you, 'A servant is not

---

31 Learn more at https://hisglory.tv/beyond-the-border.

greater than his master.' If they persecuted Me, they will also perse-cute you."

As God kept growing the reach of His Glory, the target on my back kept growing too. Even though the end of the story is already set in stone, the Enemy doesn't want our Lord to win. He'll do anything to take out those of us fighting on the Lord's behalf. For instance, in addition to the death threats we received via social media and our online platform, I've suffered multiple poisonings that I believe were purposeful.

In one instance in Tulsa in 2021, I became the sickest I've ever been in my life. And I don't use that phrase casually. It felt *even worse* than my long bout with botulism poisoning. I know that may be hard to believe, but I distinctly remember thinking: *How could this be worse than what I've already endured?* Of course, the botulism poison weak-ened me, so I was likely even more susceptible to catastrophic effects of future poisonings. But I certainly never thought I'd suffer from another poisoning in my lifetime, much less multiple episodes of it.

I'm not sharing specific details of how the poisoning occurred because it may cause panic. Multiple people from that event went into intensive care. Through the care of frontline doctors, I was able to recover. I'm just grateful to God that, yet again, he had my back—target and all.

A year earlier, our family traveled to California to visit with followers of His Glory on the West Coast. One day, we met up with a few people who watched our show *Take 5* and had long been praying for our ministry. We all went to the Standard Hotel in downtown Los Angeles to pray over it. As a Hollywood-area hotel, it represented the mountain of entertainment that the Enemy has such a strong encampment upon. I remember a dark and eerie feeling as we prayed, and I could see demonic forces within the building. As we finished praying, a light shined on the hotel.

Maybe our prayers led to what happened next.

My family traveled back to the vacation rental home we were staying in on the beach and near Camp Pendleton. Christine and the kids, aside from Creed, left to go do something fun. Creed played a game in a back bedroom. I stood on the deck overlooking the ocean, taking in God's creation. Then I glanced to my right and suddenly heard, "Look towards Camp Pendleton."

I saw a black helicopter making a beeline for me.

Two men with rifles sat at the ready, one dangling out of the left side and the other on the right side.

I ran inside.

My phone pinged.

I picked it up and saw a text message from one of my trusted military intel sources: "Your security has been breached. We're trying to help you stay clear."

I went to Creed to ensure he was safe, and we waited to see what would happen.

Nothing did.

In fact, when an investigator came to check our house the following day, looking for evidence that two white cars had rolled up to the house we were staying at, the security cameras showed nothing. The footage had been wiped.

But I'll never be able to wipe the memory of a black helicopter, rifles pointing from each side, coming directly toward me over the Pacific Ocean. I thank God for his protection and for the men and women he calls to protect others.

In 2021, I suffered another debilitating attack by the Enemy that I thought was surely going to kill me. In the middle of the night on July 3, I began to shake violently. My temperature fluctuated wildly. My anxiety skyrocketed. It felt like a heart attack—and it lasted for twelve hours.

Because I was in such a bad state, Christine started a prayer chain. I refused to go to the ER at this time as well because I'd known too many people who'd gone to the ER and hadn't returned. Plus, I recalled the last time I'd visited the ER and didn't want to repeat that experience.

During the worst of it, I felt myself above my bed by about five feet. But it was only for a moment. My fever broke. The sickness passed. The prayers had been heard. I was so exhausted by the ordeal that I slept for what felt like nearly three full days.

Because of that and the multiple poisonings I've suffered, I still fight today with my energy levels. But I'm always reminded of God's word to the apostle Paul when I think about my weakness:

And lest I should be exalted above measure by the abundance of the revelations, a thorn in the flesh was given to me, a messenger of Satan to buffet me, lest I be exalted above measure. Concerning this thing I pleaded with the Lord three times that it might depart from me. And He said to me, "My grace is sufficient for you, for My strength is made perfect in weakness." Therefore most gladly I will rather boast in my infirmities, that the power of Christ may rest upon me. Therefore I take pleasure in infirmities, in reproaches, in needs, in persecutions, in distresses, for Christ's sake. For when I am weak, then I am strong. (2 Corinthians 12:7–10)

A few days after recovering from that supposed heart attack, I spoke with my friend Dr. Richard Bartlett. I shared with him what I'd just endured. He replied that he'd just suffered from the same debilitating symptoms. He'd fallen down in front of his family, and they'd rushed him to the ER.

We hadn't been together recently. In fact, at the time, he was in Texas and I was in Ohio. So it wasn't a bug that either of us had caught. Dr. Bartlett and I both believed our sickness was caused by a heart attack drone on purpose. Like me, Dr. Bartlett had also faced multiple death threats in his work. So it wasn't surprising to either of us that we were targeted in this way. But we also weren't surprised that the prayer warriors who surrounded us ultimately helped us recover too.

Even after all of these tribulations, I come back to God's truth: "Who shall separate us from the love of Christ? Shall tribulation, or distress, or persecution, or famine, or nakedness, or peril, or sword? As it is written: 'For Your sake we are killed all day long; We are accounted as sheep for the slaughter.' Yet in all these things we are more than conquerors through Him who loved us" (Romans 8:35–37).

In January of 2017, I was meditating with the Lord and he revealed to me that our country was about to experience the greatest scandals in its history. Not just one scandal or a handful, but seventeen scandals, some of which are happening today and some of which are still to come. I believe he brought these to my attention so that we could expose them to his light at His Glory.

In fact, many of the people we've interviewed for His Glory shows have been witnesses to these scandals. For instance, Cheryl Atkinson,

Lara Logan, and General McInerney (a dear friend of mine) have all discussed the ramifications of Benghazi with me on air.

The full list of the seventeen scandals that the Lord revealed to me includes:

1. 9/11
2. Benghazi
3. State Department Pedophilia
4. Clinton Scandals
5. Clinton Foundation
6. Fast and Furious
7. IRS Scandal
8. Spy Gate / FISA unmasking
9. Fulsome
10. Hammer / Score Card
11. Uranium One
12. Fed Reserve
13. Deep State / Illuminati
14. Reagan / JFK
15. United Nations
16. Catholic Church
17. NXIVM / Epstein child

These seventeen scandals are currently in play and exposure is coming to every one of them.

CHAPTER 18

CONCLUSION

"Then David danced before the Lord with all his might."
—2 SAMUEL 6:14

Christine and I have very different tastes in music, but one group we could always agree upon is Creed. We both appreciated their style of music, but we more appreciated that they willingly chose to sing about God on some of the largest stages in the world.

In fact, we liked the group so much that both of our boys' names are based on the band. Obviously, our youngest son is directly named Creed. While that was primarily motivated by my grandfather supernaturally telling us to name him Creed, it's also a nod to our creedal statement of faith in God—and the band Creed.

Before he was born, Christine and I couldn't land on a name for our older son. Then we remembered that Scott Stapp's firstborn son was named Jagger. We both thought that was a great name. And so that's how our sons came to be named Jagger and Creed.

In addition to the inspiration for their names, I also owe Creed a deep word of thanks for providing the soundtrack I needed during our first trial and tribulation, when my marriage to Christine was at its lowest point. During that time, I listened to Creed's song "Don't Stop Dancing" hundreds of times. When you put this book down, I encourage you to listen to the song and to find and read the lyrics online.

The song's theme is exactly what I needed during that tumultuous time in my life. It may be how the Lord encourages you right now. At its core, "Don't Stop Dancing" reminds us never to quit, no matter how bad life seems. To me, I always interpreted "dancing" as our "dance" with the Lord, our daily walk with our Father.

Believe that the Lord, who knows the very number of hairs on your head, has not forgotten you. Turn to him in your joy and in your sorrow. Just don't stop dancing with him.

In his time, he will renew all. I believe we're heading into a Joel 2 movement where there's going to be the greatest revival in the history of the world. As that prophet of old wrote:

> I will pour out My Spirit on all flesh; Your sons and your daughters shall prophesy, Your old men shall dream dreams, Your young men shall see visions. And also on My menservants and on My maidservants I will pour out My Spirit in those days. And I will show wonders in the heavens and in the earth: Blood and fire and pillars of smoke. The sun shall be turned into darkness, And the moon into blood, Before the coming of the great and awesome day of the Lord. And it shall come to pass That whoever calls on the name of the Lord Shall be saved. (Joel 2:28–32)

Until the time that the Lord makes everything right, trials and tribulations will surely come into our lives, and often unexpectedly.

But for those who believe in the Lord, his light will always be there for us. No matter the depth of our pain and sorrow, he will always grant us the hope to carry on if we simply believe him at his word. Isaiah 40:31 vividly paints this picture: "Those who wait on the Lord Shall renew their strength; They shall mount up with wings like eagles, They shall run and not be weary, They shall walk and not faint."

You could even call it a dance.

As I finished the writing of this book, my mother received this prophetic word on May 2, 2024:

The Lord preserves all who love Him. He will fulfill the desire of those who fear him; he will hear their cry and save them (Psalm 145:19–21).

My Little One,

I see the exhaustion, the weariness, the battle, but know I AM is with you. Did I not say the battle is mine? Even in the fiercest battle, I AM is there.

My beloveds, breakthroughs are coming! Breakthrough for finances, breakthrough for illness, breakthroughs against the enemy's lines! Breakthrough for this movie, and breakthrough for your book, David.

I will hold you up on eagles wings, they shall run and not be weary, and they shall walk and not be faint. I AM pouring My refreshing over you. Drink Me in David, for this is the time for breakthrough. You have worked hard and diligently for My sake, and I will NOT LET YOU DOWN.

Victory is ours, the battle is turning! Watch and see My son what I AM about to do! Didn't I tell you, expect the unexpected? It is coming! Have no fear, I AM is not about to lose this ministry! I will supply ALL your needs and more. You will be overwhelmed with My provision!

I need you My son for the final harvest. You are a marine, you will be strong and courageous as Joshua and Caleb. David of the end times, preaching the truth of the Word of God. Blessings are coming My son! This darkness will flee, as My glory and judgment come upon the earth.

I began this book with Job 1:21: "The Lord gave, and the Lord has taken away; Blessed be the name of the Lord."

If you've read this far, I pray that you've seen, heard, and experienced how the Lord has given me so much and removed so much from me—all for his glory. I pray that my faithfulness to God and to his calling on my life has been apparent, even when I doubted him so often during my many wilderness years.

Again, I say none of this to boast in myself. No one else but God could have saved my marriage. No one else but God could have saved me from death—and multiple times, at that. No one else but God could have called a chronic workaholic into a ministry with a worldwide reach.

Blessed be the name of the Lord!

Remember: God loves you. Heaven is real. He wants to meet you there. But he has a great purpose for your life right now.

Are you ready?

ABOUT HIS GLORY

From east to west, north to south, we are spreading God's Word to the world and helping to restore freedom to We the People. His Glory gives a platform to pastors, prophetic voices, military leaders, politicians, and other brave patriots who are on the front lines fighting for God, truth, freedom, and justice.

Through our daily programs, our annual revival tours, and with the help of our partners, we are delivering biblical teachings, prayer, real news, interviews, and testimonies from warriors on the front lines fighting for the future of the free world.

We empower our viewers to utilize our God-given authority that is rightfully ours as children of the Most High God for such a time as this, along with the knowledge, wisdom, and discernment that comes from the Bible, and to be inspired and empowered by powerful soul-shaking testimonies from fellow His Glory warriors.

We hope our ministry blesses you and your family and remember to put on the full armor of God, so that when the day of evil comes, you may be able to stand your ground, and after you have done everything . . . to stand. (Ephesians 6:13).

We stand for God, freedom, justice, and truth. God's got this. Light wins!

Join us at HisGlory.me.

Our Purpose

Our purpose is to spread the gospel from east to west to north to south, bringing the Word of His Glory to the world and allowing the His Glory family to find community and grow in their faith.

Our Vision

Our vision is to reach a billion people worldwide with the hope of the gospel message and the truth of Jesus Christ.

Our Mission

Our mission is to equip those who seek to bring light into the darkness, to perform prayer and baptism to those who are called, to provide a platform to censored voices, and to support the poor around the globe with Bibles, food, and clothing.

Our beliefs

- The Bible is the literal and infallible Word of God.
- My house shall be called a house of prayer. Prayer is the foundation of this ministry.
- We are led by the Holy Spirit and the gifts of the Spirit.
- We have the Father's Heart for the lost, the poor, the elderly, the widow, and the orphans.
- We will be called the servants of the Most High God. We are here to serve him in ministry.
- In everything we do, we glorify our Lord. It is our love for him that compels us.
- Fivefold ministry according to Ephesians 4:11 - the apostles, prophets, evangelists, pastors, and teachers.

ABOUT DAVE SCARLETT

DAVID SCARLETT is a Chairman and Founder at His Glory, based in Valley City, Ohio. He has a diverse background, previously serving as a Global Director of Wireless Sales at Micro Vision, and also holding Director positions at notable companies like AT&T, Verizon, and Office Max. David has a Bachelor of Business Administration degree from Almeda, showcasing his educational foundation in business.

Scarlett's journey to founding His Glory was not a conventional one. He came to the Word after a near-death experience that gave him a taste of heaven and a vision of Jesus. This profound experience led him to form His Glory Ministry, aiming to bring "the Word of His Glory to the world." Through his trials and tribulations, David found love and redemption, which he now shares with others through his ministry. His Glory focuses on saving the lost and providing for the elderly and the poor, with a viewership of 25 million strong.

David's commitment to his ministry is evident through the support he provides to those on the frontline of current and spiritual events, offering biblical teachings and support to Christ followers around the world and to patriots who stand for truth, freedom, and justice.

APPENDIX

Prophetic Words

In the following pages, you'll read many of my mother's prophetic words that she received over the course of my trials. I only included a sampling within the book. She still receives these words from the Lord today, and she still shares them with me.

I am and will forever be grateful to her for who she is as a mother and who she is a spiritual prayer warrior.

THE SECOND TRIAL

August 4, 2007

"If you believe, you will receive whatever you ask for in prayer."

—MATTHEW 21:22

My Son,

Look to me for nourishment, for I will supply you with rivers of life. I came to give life, and give it abundantly. I AM the creator of life. Fill your heart with the knowing that I walk beside you, and I have your highest good in mind. Jer. 29:11: "I know the plans I have for you, plans not to harm you, but to prosper you, to give you hope and a future." Stand on my Word. When discouragement comes, remember my words for they are life. By my stripes you are healed. I carried all your infirmities and diseases on the cross. Claim all in my name. I love you.

August 6, 2007

"Save us and help us with your right hand, that those you love may be delivered."

—PSALM 108:6

My Son,

You have suffered much for my name's sake. Yet you have been faithful to me. I test my people to see who comes out strongest in the fiery furnace. You, my son, have done well. I know you are one that I can rely on. This is your time of pressing in and knowing me more. My hand is on your circumstances. Watch and see how your Lord will deliver you. If God is on your side, who can be against you? For I AM the holy one, and no one can come against my will. Yes, I have a purpose ... which you will know in time. I surround you daily with my presence. You are ever close to my heart. Healing is coming, each day stronger, each day closer to my divine plan. "I lift you up on eagle's wings, you will run and not grow weary, you will walk and not be faint." Each day, stronger, each day closer to me. I love you with an everlasting love, David. You are my son in who I am well pleased.

August 20, 2007

"Sow for yourselves righteousness, reap the fruit of
unfailing love, and break up your unplowed ground;
for it is time to seek the Lord, until he comes."

—HOSEA 10:12

My Son,

My hand is ever upon you, even in your discouragement. Remember to give me each day, trust in me. Have I ever failed you? Take baby steps, and your healing will come. Have I not said I have a purpose for your life? I will surely use you, as you have proved yourself for me. Soak in my Word, as a sponge soaks in water. If you wish to know me, know my Word. Have faith, David. You are one of my warriors, so you must put up your shield against the enemy. He knows the plans I have for you. Pray for a hedge of protection each day. Each day I will be with you. Be strong and courageous as Joshua and Caleb were. In time you will see the wholeness of my plan. You have a heart that loves your God, and your love of me will reach many. I will open and close doors of opportunity. Seek me for direction. My son, I have picked you before time, and you are one of mine. Don't fear. Trust in me, for love overcomes fear. Put your fear behind you and put love first. Watch and see how love will uplift and encourage you. I am with you.

August 21, 2007

> *"And I pray that you, being rooted and established in love, may have power, together with all the saints, to grasp how wide and long and high and deep is the love of Christ, and to know this love that surpasses knowledge ... that you may be filled to the measure of all the fullness of God."*
> —EPHESIANS 3:17–19

My Son,

See my handiwork? Have I not said I am with you? Each day I surround you with my presence. Each day letting you breathe in my love. My love will strengthen, my love will never go away. For you are one of the redeemed, my love will be everlasting. Do you love me, my son? Lo, I will never forsake you, for I have you in the palm of my hand. The only thing I ask is for you to trust me. Abraham trusted me, and it was credited to him as righteousness. Have faith in your God, nothing is impossible for me. I raise up world leaders, I bring them down. My hand is on everything. If you seek me, I will surely answer. Time is short, I need my warriors for the end-time outpouring. I will restore, I will bless, I will favor you my son as I AM the God of restoration. Time for blessings. I will open the doors of heaven for you.

August 22, 2007

> *"He will bring glory to me by taking from what is mine, and making it known to you. All that belongs to*

the Father is mine. That is why I said the spirit will
take from what is mine and make it known to you."

—JOHN 16:14

My Son,

It is true my son. I give you my spirit that will make known all of my knowledge. You will see and understand my Word, where the world will be confounded. They will see, but not understand. I give you understanding. For the secrets of the kingdom are riches you cannot buy on earth. These riches I give you. Walk in the spirit, and the spirit will guide, the spirit will reveal. Healing is coming, and you will be restored, but a new man you will be. A man of spirit, not a man of the world. What a difference you will make when you walk in the spirit and are obedient to my Word. Begin to learn my Word. I will show you many things. My son, have I not been there with you? Have I not been faithful? Again I say, trust and let me lead you. For I will bring you much joy and a hope that is eternal. Give that hope to others. I love you.

August 27, 2007

"Jesus replied, 'Love the Lord your god with all your heart, and with
all your soul, and with all your mind. This is the first and greatest
commandment. And the second is like it, "Love your neighbor as your-
self." All the law and the prophets hang on these two commandments."

—MATTHEW 22:37–39

My son,

Have I not been faithful to you? You have seen how I uplift my redeemed and desire an intimate relationship with them. You are my bride, and I am your groom. Doesn't love permeate our relationship? Love is what binds us together, and love endures forever. Is not love the greatest of the commandments? You have seen my love and the love of others, David, by me and by others. Use this love in a positive way—reach others for me so that they can experience this love. It is everlasting, for I have said, "I will never leave you or forsake you." You are mine for eternity. As I begin to bless you, bless others. For my spiritual law says you reap what you sow. Sow love, it will come back. Sow money, and it will return to you. It is like a garden: the more you sow, the more you produce. Produce much in my name, David. Seek me always. For those who seek me will find me. You will see my favor upon you in the months ahead. "For surely, O Lord, you bless the righteous, you surround them with your favor as a shield." I AM your shield my son.

THE THIRD TRIAL

October 25, 2014

Hold fast what you have that no one may take your crown.

My Daughter,

I see how you long for my will and look to me for guidance. Can I the Living God not provide for you? Resources are coming. Do not go ahead of me. Trust that I will open the door.

You look to me for an answer whether to write a book. Have I put it on your heart so that you cannot shake it? Is there an unction to do so? Seek me in this. Have I not told you that His Glory will glorify my name? The Holy Spirit will guide you and you will feel led.

David will know in his spirit what he is to do. The unction will not leave him until my purpose is completed. Keep growing in me, Debbie. There is much ahead of you and you will be overwhelmed! Take one day at a time. The Spirit will lead. And know that my hand is on you both. I AM is working on family. Look to me the author and finisher of your faith. A huge windfall is coming—be prepared. For suddenly you will be thrust out into ministry.

Enjoy the quiet times with me. Come often and sit at my feet as Mary did. Soak up my presence and my love. Love will abound wherever you go. People will see me in you—as I am in the Father, so you are in me. Abide little one—your future will unfold as naturally as a baby's birth. It is a progression—each level more teaching, more understanding, more revelation.

I love you dearly and I AM will complete the purpose I have ordained in you and David's ministry! Be filled with joy as you will be entwined with my desire. I am cutting loose all earthly ties—you are seeking the kingdom's treasures now. Go in *love,* for this is what will bring many to me—love. Love people. Love is your mantle.

Learn all from me as I know abide with you. My hand will guide and your feet will follow my divine plan. Be at peace my daughter—I have this!

February 6, 2015

> *I have glorified you on the earth. My food is to do the will*
> *of him who sent me and to finish his work (John 17:4).*

My Daughter,

You are now the ones to finish the work I have started. Would I not finish the work I have ordained? Stand on faith my daughter. Your God will supply all your needs according to your riches in Christ Jesus. My purpose will stand, and your destinies will be fulfilled. Watch and see the power and glory of your God. His Glory is my ministry—for My Glory. It will accomplish all that I desire it to be. Have not other pastors joined your cause? Fear not about David's disability—have I not sustained you this far? Is my arm too short to save? Watch and be sure I AM is ready to fulfill all that I have purposed. It shall stand and no weapon formed against it shall stand. The doors are beginning to open and I AM will lead you as I led Moses to the people of Israel.

Yes, Debbie, we are in the time of the end, but the great outpouring will fall soon upon my people. Humble yourself as you must be ready to handle the power with great humility and wisdom. Daughter, I see your heart . . . your children will be covered and will know how much you love them and pray for them. I know life has thrown many trials at you, but that is why you are readying yourself for the ministry to come. Nothing comes by chance when my hand guides. Love will abound as you continue to seek my face.

June 5, 2015

Because you speak this word, behold, I will make my words in your mouth fire, and this people wood, and it shall devour them.

My daughter,

How I have longed for you as many things have taken your attention. Now is the time, you must focus more on me and the direction I am leading you too. Did I not prepare His Glory and ready it for this time? Can your God not supply all your needs? Faith, little one, my arm is not too short to save. I have never left you, but continue to put my hand on your ministry. The doors will open, and David will know what he is to do. You wonder about a godly man to be part of the ministry. Can not the I AM touch a heart and lead a person to this ministry? I know, Debbie, that you want to be certain that this is my plan, not yours. You always seek my faith and ask for counsel. That's why I trust you for this ministry. It is all to my glory, and you and David have a servant's heart. Did Noah doubt when he made the ark? Did Abraham refuse to leave his home? They knew that I was with them, orchestrating the way. So it is with you. I AM is orchestrating the way. You will know that you know when things fall into place. My light will shine in the darkness and many will come in. As for you, my daughter, remain where you are, but get ready for things ahead. I have mighty plans ahead. I love you so my daughter.

January 2016

My daughter,

I hear your cry for your precious son and wife. I AM God, can I not handle this situation? Again you have put your trust in me. Again I will say, "Those who put their trust in me will not be put to shame." Truth will prevail, and My hand will be on their situation. Do I not know every heart? Is not my heart for Jagger? Stand back and let I AM ACT! Enough is enough! I have declared it and I will perform it. Did you not see the cardinal today? Trust in me for have I not carried you this far? I see the pain, the worry, but did I not say, "Cast all your anxieties on me for I care for you"? My son, you have listened and obeyed. You are my servant whom I trust. Watch how I, the Lord, fights for you. Did you not see miracles in Liberia? It is time for me to ACT! Blessings are coming, and I will deal with the [other family]! I will hedge up and expose. Be still before me, and I will show you the way. Satan is frantic, as this ministry will bless many in MY NAME! Know, my beloveds, you are loved and valued by your God!

February 25, 2016

My Child,

My beloved, oh how I have longed for your surrender of your heart. I rejoice at the love you have for me. Yes, I have molded you and are still working on those areas of sin which you are not even aware of. My joy is that you have received this with great acceptance as your heart longs to serve and be obedient to me. Humility again is a must, and the Holy Spirit will lead you in this and will check your spirit if pride arises. Love is the center of my core, and it is the heart of every ministry. My love will overflow to others as you soak me in.

People will be drawn to the love of Christ within you. Daughter, be at peace as I will deliver Dave and Christine and your ministry. They have taken bold steps to glorify my name. Nothing will stop me from being glorified! My will will go forth and my abundance will be at your disposal. Am I a God of unlimited resources? You will see my abundance in a time of lack. Hold fast to me and bind my Word to the tablet of your heart! You will be blessed and I will rejoice over you with singing! You are so loved, beloved . . . you are mine, and my precious jewel. Forever you will be with me in my kingdom—my glorious bride.

April 1, 2016

My child,

I see how you grieve over the events in your life. The loss of a loved one is so painful. Debbie, be of good cheer, Cody is with me, safe at peace, and cherished and loved in heaven. Yes, hearts are broken because he left an imprint on loving others. His heart so wanted family unity, love, and understanding. I AM is in your midst. I have NOT forgotten you, and I know how you must struggle. Your heart is so tender for my ministry, and question why is this happening to David? Why does he need to be assaulted with evil?

My precious one, did you forget that I your God can do anything? That every step of your journey is pre-planned by me to prepare for you your purpose to be fulfilled and my name glorified? Dave's story is not over, he will see the supply of his God. I have tested him and found him faithful. I must have a servant who is obedient to my voice. He has proved that, and now he must listen to my voice, and I will lead him. Though things look dark now, my light will shine forth like the morning sun. He will know that he knows my voice and what he must do. I am readying him for my purpose and my plan. Though you see things that seem overwhelming my hand is upon it. There is a reason for everything. I will tell David what he is to do. As I have told you, his story is not finished—Have I not supplied his needs this far? Did I not give Joseph the authority and wealth of Egypt? Can I not rescue with my right hand? Though you cannot see now, a great future awaits you. The desires of your hearts will be fulfilled. Your question of selling his house—wait on me, wait on me and seek my face, and you will know without a doubt what I desire you to do. You have been tested in the furnace, and I know that I can trust you as I trusted Abraham. Did I not say my purpose will stand? Did I not bring you this far, for my glory? Step back and see my hand work daughter. Things are going to explode, and your family will see the truth of my Word and that the God you love will supply! They will see and know you are favored by the Most High. Be at peace. I have never left you or David, and you will see the Glory of God in the land of the living! My name will be glorified, and you, my daughter, will see the blessing of your God. I AM is with you, not against you. I give you a future and a hope. Did I not say that those who put their trust in me will never be put to shame? You are covered by the Most High. The raindrops are starting, and soon an outpouring. Be ready to receive, keep in the Word and close to my heart. My sheep know My voice and you will clearly know what to do. I love you, my daughter. Never fear but trust the one who is going before you.

March 2, 2016

My child,

Listen to the call of nature. Is not my glory in this? Yes, daughter I AM is everywhere, I AM is pleased that you seek my counsel. You have always turned to the voice of truth. Am I not capable of provision? I will supply all your needs according to my riches in Christ Jesus. I know you seek my direction concerning the insurance company. Again David will be led by the Spirit. He will have confirmation in what he needs to do. My voice will be clear to him. Have I not guided him so far? Look at what he has accomplished so far, by hearing my voice. My timing is always right, and soon things will be happening to bless and supply. It will happen quickly, and he will know I AM is in control. My ministry will not be touched or no man will come against it. I have purposed it and it will stand! Watch and see my hand on His Glory for it is mine say that the Lord. What is an insurance company to me? I AM the provider of wealth. All wealth comes through my hand. Blessings will follow you, wherever you go, and people will see the favor of your God.

June 26, 2016

"If you abide in my word, you are my disciples indeed. And you shall know the truth, and the truth will set you free."

—JOHN 8:31–32

My Child,

I see the busyness of your life right now. It is okay, Debbie. Know that I AM with you. You will find that precious time you spend with me, for I know daughter how much you *love* me. You have waited patiently, always turning to me for guidance. I will guide and *lead* you to where I want you to go.

The ministry is on the brink of a great outpouring! It will happen quickly and your lives will be forever changed. My ministry will reach the world, and MY GLORY will be known. Many signs and wonders will accompany you in MY ministry. It will bring much glory to My name!

Humility is a must, more time with Scripture, prayer, and healing. Seek me early and I will bless. David will see clearly the plans I have for him. Yes, confirmation will always lead you to the right path.

Never fear, little one, I HAVE THIS! Just be obedient and listen to my voice.

David's house will sell and things will begin happening. You will be amazed how I supply! Never fear, dear heart, the church in Liberia will be built. It is not a mistake that I chose that place first. It is all in My plan.

Be prepared for an exciting ministry which will bring in many. You have longed to serve me and I know your servant's heart. Get in physical shape, watch your diet, and get ready to serve. Don't worry about your husband, the farm, I will show you the way. Have you always turned to me? I love you, my daughter!

September 26, 2016

> *"I will greatly rejoice in the Lord, my soul shall be joyful in my God. For he has clothed my with the garments of salvation. He has covered me with the robe of righteousness."*
>
> —ISAIAH 61:10

My daughter,

You have waited for me, and I will *act* when my timing is right. You have put your faith in me and my timing which has put you at ease. You know that I will go before you and that doors will be opened that have been closed. Opportunities will begin flowing and His Glory will be sent out. For My Name is Great, and you have humbly put me first in everything.

Draw near to me, Debbie, and I will draw *near* to you. Call to me and I will answer and show you great and unsearchable things. Am I not the Lord God? What is it that I cannot do? Only one thing, and that is forcing men to choose me and my son. Is this not my heart's desire that salvation is for everyone? My house awaits those who love me, but there is room for all! My heart aches at the many who are blinded by the world and whose hearts are hardened. Like Pharoah, they *refuse* to obey and come against my Holy One!

Take one step, then another, and soon a pathway will be formed. I have you by my hand, and you will step into your ordained destiny. I will never let go until, my daughter, I bring you home. More of me, more of times of intimacy, more times of prayer. Prayer is the key to breakthrough in every situation.

Daughter, joy in this, your God *will* supply all your needs according to the riches in Christ Jesus. Your ministry will overflow with an abundance of resources. His Glory nations will abide in much power. You will see your son accomplishing much in My Name. My Glory will be spread over all the earth.

You will heal in My Name—giving me the Glory! Joy will be unspeakable as you see me at work. I, the Lord, will do it. Soon, little one, you will be stepping out with confidence and boldness, knowing it is I that sustains you. Soak me in, imprint my Word on your heart. Love is my name, daughter. All is well. Go in *peace*, knowing that your God has it in control.

January 4, 2017

"The Lord your God is in your midst. The mighty one will save. He will rejoice over you with gladness. He will quiet you with his love. He will rejoice over you with singing."
—ZEPHANIAH 3:16

My Child,

Oh, how my heart yearns for you, my gentle flower. Too much busyness, more focus on me. Fill your days with my Word, my presence and worship. Pray always, even little prayers throughout your day. Debbie, time to get serious about your physical health. You must get ready to travel. I know how you worry about your husband, your house, but put it all in my hands. Have I not been there for every trial? I have always carried you through. The time is here, 2017, a year of tribulation, but also a year of great increase. My ministry is ready to launch. You and David must be ready for it is beyond anything you can imagine. Yes, daughter, you will come out of hiding and be known. Signs and wonders will accompany you and Dave wherever you go. Seek me more often, immerse yourself in my Word, and *love* and pursue me with all of your heart. You will be amazed at what is coming. So much joy as you see my mighty hand! I will fill you with my love and you will be a beacon of light for those who are lost. The tribe of Judah, I know you would never have guessed of your son's Jewish root. David, and Deborah of the end times, glorifying My Name and bringing many to Christ. Love, love, love in My Name. Love always wins!

January 14, 2017

"And it shall happen in that day that I will make Jerusalem a very heavy stone for all peoples; all who would heave it away will surely be cut in pieces, though all nations of the earth are gathered against it."

—ZECHARIAH 12:3

My child,

Your heart rejoices with mine. As you read, Solomon knew that "I am my beloved, and my beloved is mine." That is the love I have for my church. I AM is eagerly awaiting the marriage supper of the Lamb. He is anxiously waiting to come to gather his bride. What joy on that day when we will be united!

Debbie, I have loved you before I placed you in your mother's womb. Know that I AM is with you. My glory will shine through the ministry of His Glory. You will be humbled at what I desire you to do. Place your trust in me, for I will *never* fail you. As I have said, those who put their trust in me will never be put to shame. Daughter, I am feeling you with my Spirit … soak in my Word and imprint it on your heart. My word will flow easily from you as you are placing the Word in your heart. Watch for the miracles in 2017! My daughter, you bring me much joy as your love for me increases. Yes, you are pursuing *me* and *loving* my Word too! *Time* is short, many things are coming about in 2017. Some tribulations, but also much favor and increase for my church. I AM is looking for the Church of Philadelphia! Be sacrificial, striving for holiness, and filled with my agape *love*! Your love of me will attract *many* who are searching for meaning in their lives. Their purpose is a spiritual one, not worldly. They must realize that earth is temporary, but heaven or hell is eternal. No going back to change their decisions made on earth. Tell them, my little one, choose this day whom you will serve, mammon or the Most High?

February 22, 2017

"Learn to do good; Seek justice, Rebuke the oppressor;
Defend the fatherless, Plead for the widow."
—ISAIAH 1:17

My daughter,

Oh I see your love of me through MY WORD! Yes, Debbie, I will imprint it on the tablet of your heart, for you are mine saith the Lord. Think not I have not yet moved as my timing is always right. *Trust* little one I have the battle plan. You must be obedient and obey what I AM telling you. Open your ears to hear the *Word* of the Lord. I know how much you love my beloved city, and I know it is because I dwell there. But I have set my peg in that place, a holy, sacred place where I will always dwell. Daughter, can I not arrange a leader or a nation to fall in a day? Is orchestrating this ministry an easy thing for me? Again I say, I *have* the plan, you must trust to be obedient. Did Joseph know fully my plan for him, or Abraham? This is the end days, and you and David are *called*! I will ordain your feet, and you will touch others for My Name's sake! I will do it saith the Lord! Don't be like Sarah and laugh because of age. I will strengthen and uphold you for the task. Jerusalem, my Jerusalem, yes a His Glory ministry.

May 25, 2017

"The Lord, the Lord is my strength and
my song, he has become my salvation."
—ISAIAH 12:2

My daughter,

My little one, how I long for our marriage feast, but first we have the final harvest. I see how tender you are as a soul is brought into the kingdom. I see how you love my Word as it sanctifies you, my daughter. You will be My bride spotless without wrinkle. You and David have touched many lives for My name's sake. This is only the tip of the iceberg. A flood is coming . . . get ready, get ready for I AM is about to launch a mighty ministry. You laugh at your budget and lack of donations. Watch My hand, I will provide. My servant David is pleasing to me. I see his heart and passion. I will use this passionate heart to reach many in My name. You have honored me by making My name known and not your own. Blessings will come because of it. I know you wonder how we will continue with lack of funds. This is nothing for Me. Am I not the provider? Have I not sustained you so far? I will be your provider. Trust and obey, that is all I ask of you. Watch, soon you will be overflowing with resources. I will bless, I will provide. You have trusted in the Most High. I will undergird your ministry in ways you cannot imagine. You are reaching my beloveds, and I will bless you for it. Stay firm on My truth, even though the world values are opposite to My Word! My Word does not change. I AM not a God who lies, but a God who speaks truth. I AM THE WAY, THE TRUTH, AND THE LIFE! So many of my beloveds have gone astray, they have not put My truth in their hearts. My heart weeps for My people to return. Be My mouthpiece, David. Bring My people home, for I long for them with all My heart.

June 7, 2017

"Love the Lord your God, with all your mind, all your strength, and all your heart, I love your neighbor as yourself."

—MARK 12:30

My daughter,

Drink me in, beloved. I AM is always at your side. You must always *trust* and obey. Isn't this what I have told you many times? You have put your trust in me, and I will *supply* all your needs. Not some, but all. I AM Jehovah Jireh, your provider. I have purposed your ministry, and I will do it! Have you lacked anything? Is not His Glory operating in the small funds I have given you? I can change a heart and increase your supply! Don't worry, dear heart, about funds and David's finances. Stand back and see your God supply! We have a ministry to launch and I AM is *ready*! You will never know the effect of this ministry on unbelievers, but I know, for I have seen it already! Rejoice, your God is using you and David to proclaim his Word and His Glory. I will send you the *right* people to help in your ministry for I know their hearts. And as for a worship team, I will send you the *right* one. I AM is working on hearts. Always, again I say always, seek my face for wisdom and counsel. Beloved, I go before you, preparing the way. It will be a glorious way! Be blessed, my daughter, your king has *heard* your cry. Supplies, resources, people *are* coming!

June 15, 2017

"But the Lord will arise over you, And His glory will be seen upon you."

—ISAIAH 60:2

My daughter,

Have you not known? It is I your savior that goes before you. I *purpose* it and it prevails. His glory will prevail with glory and Majesty! I AM that I AM. My plan will stand. Rejoice, my daughter, I have never left you. My plan will unfold quickly and suddenly. Your ministry will blossom. You have touched my heart with your love, and I want that love to bring others to Christ. Remember your favorite verse when the rest of the world seems fearful. "I can do all things through Christ who strengthens me." Sing with joy for you are mine saith the Lord. The evil one will never snatch you out of My hand. David and Deborah, My bond servants of the end times. There is no mistake that you were named after My special ones. You will receive the mantle of Deborah and David for this time. Go in My anointing, touching others for Christ! My hand is upon you. Again, trust and obey for I will lead the way. My beloveds I go with you.

August 2017

"Son of man, I have made you a watchman for the house of Israel; there-fore hear a word from My mouth and give them warning from Me."
—EZEKIEL 3:17

My little one,

Oh how my heart rejoices at the love you have for me. Yes, more prophetic words are coming. My words are reaching people all over the world. Humility is a must as this ministry grows! Am I a God who is never late? I Am is always on time. Watch and see your God provides. Am I not Jehovah Jireh, your provider? I know how you worry about finances, but dear heart, I am the creator of everything. Do you think I would not send David out after all this preparation? Dwell in the shadow of The Most High and you will hear my words and know what I am doing. His Glory nations will arise as my name is upon them. Soak me in as you continue to study, as in the days ahead you will be used. No preparation is enough without My Spirit.

The Holy Spirit will teach and lead you into all truth. Time is in my hands daughter, and I Am is aware of David's finances. You need only to trust and obey as this is paramount to going forth in this ministry. I Am is sending you help. As you have always sought my face, this ministry will be led by me. People will know it is my anointing and My Glory will be established on the earth. Be diligent in your studies and I will fill you with my agape love and My healing power. David will be my spokesman in great power and authority. He is humbled as Paul and zealous for my kingdom. Love is my banner for it is out of love that I gave my son so that we could be reconciled forever. Watch current events. 2017 will be explosive and it will also be a tremendous outpouring of My Spirit. I will provide, little one.

August 10, 2017
Word to Dave

Thus says the Lord, the World is shaking by my hands. Did I not tell my Prophets of these days? North Korea will be SHAKEN by ME. A great revival will come to Korea in my Name. Tell my people to Trust ME in ALL things as I have the keys of DAVID! I AM is ready to Launch HIS Ministry with great anointing and Power and the World will see Signs and Wonders of HIS GLORY!

August 28, 2017
Word to Dave

"For your love is ever before me, and I will
walk continually in your truth."
—PSALM 26:3

The Evil one does not want what I have written to be done. See How he snatches the pen out of the air? Do you not think I have this! I AM is in control! He the evil one is frantic over this ministry called by my name HIS GLORY. He is trying to rob you of your mantle and my love and call for you and your family. Satan has come against my beloveds to try to intimidate and distract you BUT this will backfire as I AM is using this to drive my Glory to the World. I have seen the suffering of your beloved Mother, She is called for this Time! She WILL pray with power and anointing and the Evil one will not stop it. Your beloved wife is searching and seeking my heart and face and she will find me and I AM is setting her on a path to know me intimately and I AM is healing her for my Glory! My Glory will shine on the World through HIS GLORY and no weapon ever formed will stop it. My Creed, oh I AM is pleased with his Loving faithful heart. He will be used for my Glory! My Son, it is the time that I prepared you for and you have listened and obeyed. Now watch! Expect the unexpected! I AM is ready for my Ministry.

October 12, 2017

"I cried out to the Lord because of my affliction, and He answered me. Out of the belly of Sheol I cried, and You heard my voice."

— JONAH 2:2

My dearest child,

I heard your cry in prayer has reached my heavenly throne. I know your heart and how much you want to serve me. Debbie, I AM is for you, not against you. This too will pass and I will strengthen you and show you your destiny. You must set your house in shape for I AM is sending you out. I know the love you have for me and I will open and close your doors. It is good you fill your heart with my Word and grow to know me more. Little one, your love brings great joy and love of service to me. Light a beacon to others so my love can be felt. Time is shortened. As I said, more tribulations. Your blessing is coming. Stay encouraged. I have supplied. I know how proud of David you are and how it has brought so much joy to you.

He is passionate and I will bless. He is my Paul, determined to reach others for my name's sake. Love is at the core of everything that you learn today. Are you motivated by love? Oh Debbie, I so much want to show you what lies ahead for my beloveds. As Scripture says, no eye has seen, no ear has heard or mind conceived what I have in store for those who love me. You are one of my beloveds taking joy in knowing your future. You will be united with me for all eternity. I love you, my daughter.

November 27, 2017

"Grass withers and flowers fade,
but the word of our God stands forever."
—ISAIAH 40:8

My Child,

I see your frustration but, little one, patience is a virtue. Be patient and know that I your Lord have everything in My hands. Are My arms too short to save? Nothing is impossible for ME! Be faithful and obedient, and I will supply all your needs! Do you think I would let My ministry fail? TRUST in this hour . . . know that the doors of heaven are opening and My beloveds will be blessed! You ask for nothing for self but for My ministry to go forth! It will not FAIL! For My hand, the almighty is upon it. Have I not led you this far? Do you think I would fail you now? Take joy, stand in faith, to receive all that I have promised. My glory will be exalted throughout the nation. Watch and see what I Am is doing! Have I not increased numbers? I know your financial situation. I will tell you exactly what I want you to do! You are My beloveds, I see the heart of love for Me and others! David, you are anointed with My heart, and signs and wonders will follow you and bring in many. Debbie, think not you are too old. Your anointing is healing in My name. Many will believe because of this miraculous healing! I will give you the energy to go out and the joy of seeing My hand will create such exuberance that you will not think of an aging body. Time is closing in, My saints must collect the harvest. Know that I will always supply. I love you both so much as I see your hearts are for ME! Be blessed in My name.

Date unknown

My hand is upon Christine. My presence will be with her. I will move her heart and she will know I AM the Living God! I will rescue, I will save. There is always a consequence to sin, but after repentance there is restoration. I am restoring her to a relationship with me and a relationship with her family. She is in my hand and I walk with her wherever she goes. You have surrendered your family to me. Watch and see my loving support and bounty. They will be praising me and I will use them in the end time of battle. Be courageous, Debbie, your prayers are heard. Praise your God, victory is coming!

A letter from Christine. Date unknown.

We want to give you assurance that you are all in our hearts and prayers. We love you. The Lord is our guide and we wait on him for his guidance. His time is different than ours yet we learn patience and to trust. The Lord is our father. We are his servants.

My husband, as servant, reaches many to share the message of salvation. This message he puts on his website for all to continue in their walk to getting closer to know Jesus. These messages can be encouraging, uplifting, and are meant for you and everyone. These are his ways of using what the Holy Spirit has gifted him with.

I know you are so dear to him that he wants to see you all in person again, but we wait on the Lord and trust his leading. Sometimes we are in a period of waiting and it can seem we are alone or forgotten. This is never the case. God has a plan and it is meant for good. As I reach out daily to God, I do not always feel his awesome presence yet

I know his love for me is great and he is always there. I pray that you will get encouragement and guidance from his Word and prayer. Your family and church community are very dear to our hearts—always.

In 1 Corinthians 1:17, Paul was emphasizing that no one person should do everything. Paul's gift was preaching and that's what he did. Christian ministry should be a team effort, no preacher or teacher is a complete link between God and people, and no individual can do all things. David's gift is to preach and bring people to know Christ.

Date unknown

Continue to seek time with me, Debbie . . . It is essential for your growth. More with me before you reach others. I will look over your family and I AM with Dave, Christine. Watch and see my mercy and grace. Creed will be a man of God, faithful to his God. My hand is upon him. He is special. Did I not say I was the God of restoration? David will see the goodness of the Lord. I will bless, I will restore. His heart is for me therefore I will be with him. You will see your son grow as a mighty man of God, firm in his love and allegiance to me. He will be used for my glory.

David Scarlett is a Chairman and Founder at His Glory, a ministry that reaches millions around the globe. As a United States Marine, he was stationed in Japan and traveled the world in service to the nation he loves.

David had a successful career in business, serving as a Global Director of Wireless Sales at Micro Vision, and also holding Director positions at notable companies like AT&T, Verizon, and Office Max.

Scarlett's journey to founding His Glory was not a conventional one. He came to the Word after a near-death experience that gave him a taste of Heaven and a vision of Jesus. This profound encounter led him to form His Glory, aiming to bring "the Word of His Glory to the world."

Through his trials and tribulations, David found love and redemption, which he now shares with others through his ministry. His Glory focuses on saving the lost and providing for the elderly and the poor, with a viewership of 25 million strong.

David's commitment to his ministry is evident through the support he provides to those on the frontline of current and spiritual events, offering biblical teachings and support to Christ-followers around the world, and to patriots who stand for truth, freedom, and justice.

www.HisGlory.me
www.HisGlory.TV

Join us

Follow us by subscribing to our free email newsletter, and subscribing to our video channels!

You can also help us reach one billion souls by becoming a Kingdom Builder and by joining or starting a Warrior Group.

www.HisGlory.me/Local-Groups